PSYCHOLOGY RESEARCH PROGRESS

PSYCHOLOGY OF SELF-CONTROL

PSYCHOLOGY OF EMOTIONS, MOTIVATIONS AND ACTIONS

Additional books in this series can be found on Nova's website under the Series tab.

Additional E-books in this series can be found on Nova's website under the E-book tab.

PSYCHOLOGY RESEARCH PROGRESS

Additional books in this series can be found on Nova's website under the Series tab.

Additional E-books in this series can be found on Nova's website under the E-book tab.

PSYCHOLOGY RESEARCH PROGRESS

PSYCHOLOGY OF SELF-CONTROL

AMPELIO DURANTE AND CLAUD MAMMOLITI
EDITORS

Nova Science Publishers, Inc.
New York

Copyright © 2012 by Nova Science Publishers, Inc.

For permission to use material from this book please contact us:
Telephone 631-231-7269; Fax 631-231-8175
Web Site: http://www. novapublishers. com

NOTICE TO THE READER

The Publisher has taken reasonable care in the preparation of this book, but makes no expressed or implied warranty of any kind and assumes no responsibility for any errors or omissions. No liability is assumed for incidental or consequential damages in connection with or arising out of information contained in this book. The Publisher shall not be liable for any special, consequential, or exemplary damages resulting, in whole or in part, from the readers' use of, or reliance upon, this material. Any parts of this book based on government reports are so indicated and copyright is claimed for those parts to the extent applicable to compilations of such works.

Independent verification should be sought for any data, advice or recommendations contained in this book. In addition, no responsibility is assumed by the publisher for any injury and/or damage to persons or property arising from any methods, products, instructions, ideas or otherwise contained in this publication.

This publication is designed to provide accurate and authoritative information with regard to the subject matter covered herein. It is sold with the clear understanding that the Publisher is not engaged in rendering legal or any other professional services. If legal or any other expert assistance is required, the services of a competent person should be sought. FROM A DECLARATION OF PARTICIPANTS JOINTLY ADOPTED BY A COMMITTEE OF THE AMERICAN BAR ASSOCIATION AND A COMMITTEE OF PUBLISHERS.

Additional color graphics may be available in the e-book version of this book.

LIBRARY OF CONGRESS CATALOGING-IN-PUBLICATION DATA

Psychology of self-control / editors, Ampelio Durante and Claud Mammoliti.
    p. cm.
Includes index.
ISBN 978-1-61470-881-0 (hardcover)
1. Self-control. 2. Control (Psychology) I. Durante, Ampelio. II. Mammoliti, Claud.
BF632.P778 2011
155.2'5--dc23
                2011027364

Published by Nova Science Publishers, Inc. † New York

CONTENTS

PREFACE

In this book, the authors present current research in the study of the psychology of self-control. Topics discussed include sociotropy-autonomy and self-control; a computerized detour task for the assessment of self-control behavior; a gender specific analysis of impulsivity and aggression; intuitions about self-control and the ideomotor principle; the self-management correlates of social anxiety and children's increased mental control through external cues.

Chapter 1 - It has been shown that highly sexually resourceful women utilize a variety of self-regulatory strategies to deal with unwanted sexual advances that do not involve coercion or sexual assault. What is less understood, however, is how women acquire this skill repertoire. A concurrent mixed-methods approach was used to help unfold this phenomenon. After completing inventories assessing general and sexual resourcefulness skills, nine women were interviewed about their sexual socialization experiences. Four young women, representing the four extreme combinations of scores on these inventories, were first subjected to constant comparative analysis. The substantive model of sexual resourcefulness that emerged from this analysis was further supported by three additional young cases. The substantive model illustrates that the mass media and peers are influential factors that together have a large impact on women's beliefs about relationships, beauty and body image. Women high in sexual resourcefulness did not subscribe to the values portrayed in the media and also said that their friends outright rejected the messages it conveyed. In sharp contrast, women low in sexual resourcefulness, along with their peer group, were immersed with how they looked and presented themselves in sexual situations, incessantly making comparisons with characters they identified with in the media. Implications for parents and sexual health educators are discussed. Based on the narrative of another two older women, the authors also describe why for some the development of sexual resourcefulness may come later in life.

Chapter 2 - The purpose of this chapter is to link the construct of self-control or self-regulation to a model by the same title in Relational Competence Theory (RCT; Cusinato & L'Abate, in press; L'Abate, Cusinato, Maino, Colesso, & Scilletta, 2010). Self-control, like many other ubiquitous orphan psychological constructs, such as locus of control, reactivity, resilience, and self-esteem among others, historically has not been heretofore connected usually to any specific theory in any particularly testable fashion. If and when this construct has been linked to a theory, e. g. , psychoanalysis, social learning, operant conditioning, or attachment, for instance, it has not been stated in ways that lead to empirical or experiential verification and validation, except perhaps for behavioral formulations. However, only its normative rather than non-normative aspects have been usually considered. The latter will be included here because they are an intrinsic aspect of models in RCT, especially self-report.

Chapter 3 - Research by Baumeister et al. (1998) suggests the existence of a limited source of mental energy that can be used for self-control. Personality differences, however, can influence how rapidly this mental energy is lost after engaging in tasks requiring self-control (Tangney, Baumeister, & Boone, 2004). Additionally, recent research suggests that personality differences in sociotropy and autonomy can contribute to how an individual attempts to replenish the lost mental energy (Sato, Harman, Donohoe, Weaver, & Hall, 2010). In his theory of depression, Beck (1983) suggests that individuals high in the personality dimensions of sociotropy and autonomy are at an increased risk of depression. Highly sociotropic individuals have a strong need for social acceptance and are more likely to resort to seeking help from others in stressful situations (Beck, 1983). Conversely, highly autonomous individuals tend to place great emphasis on personal accomplishments and may feel de-energized and depressed when they believe they have failed (Beck, 1987). This chapter summarizes two studies which investigate how highly sociotropic and autonomous individuals differ in their response to the loss of mental energy following tasks that require active self-control. Study 1 investigated whether individuals high in sociotropy or autonomy have less mental energy to begin with and whether they expend more mental energy when they engage in tasks that require self-control than those low in the respective personality traits. Study 2 examined how the loss of mental energy affects the motivation of individuals high in sociotropy and autonomy compared to those low in the respective personality dimensions. The results of Study 1 suggest that while highly sociotropic individuals have less mental energy to begin with than those low in sociotropy, they may not expend more mental energy while engaging in tasks requiring self-control. Study 2 revealed two interesting results. The first was that highly autonomous individuals have more motivation to perform well on personal tasks requiring self-control than individuals low in autonomy overall. The second interesting result was that highly autonomous individuals' motivation to perform well on personal tasks increases more than those low in autonomy following a task requiring high levels of self-control.

Chapter 4 - The detour task is a classic problem in which a participant must ascertain how to obtain a reward item that is placed on the opposite side of a barrier. A direct response to the reward is typically not possible and must be inhibited. Instead, the participant must move away from the reward in order to detour the barrier and ultimately gain access to the reward. Many species have proved capable of solving variations of the task, albeit in different ways and at different speeds. The authors created a novel variation of this task for presentation on a computer monitor, building upon the strengths of the original detour problem and other previous tests of self-control behavior. In two experiments, nine rhesus monkeys (*Macacamulatta*) had to detour a cursor around a bar-shaped stimulus that represented a small reward in order to reach a more distant stimulus that represented a large reward. In Experiment 1, monkeys' performance on this variation of the task was compared to a more traditional self-control test in which monkeys chose to move a cursor one of two durations/distances to select stimuli representing different size rewards. In the traditional test, all monkeys were heavily biased to the self-control (larger-further) response, whereas monkeys' performance in the detour test was more variable and positively related to age and/or experience. Older monkeys with more computerized test experience were more often willing to detour the small reward stimulus to select the large reward stimulus. In Experiment 2, they eliminated the latter relationship by training less experienced monkeys to accurately move the cursor around a non-reward barrier. Following this training, all nine monkeys were retested in the computerized detour task and all were biased to make the detour response or were indifferent between the two response options. These results indicate that this computerized detour task provides a novel assessment of self-control behavior, different from that of the traditional self-control test. Further research is needed with these and other tasks to elucidate what specific task requirements result in differential performance like that seen in the present study.

Chapter 5 - Low self-control is an important and stable predictor of offending. Low self-control is often thought of as a multidimensional trait

(Gottfredson & Hirschi, 1990). Key dimensions are impulsivity; aggression and risk-taking behaviour. The aim of this paper is to explain individual differences in low self-control as one latent construct and two of its dimensions, namely impulsivity and aggression. It is well established that low levels of self-control increase the risk of offending. However, there is less empirical research that focuses on the role of family structure and socialisation on impulsivity and aggression, two key dimensions of low-self control. Similarly, few research has posed the question to what extent such a model holds for both boys and girls. Therefore the main research question for this study is to explain to what extent family structure, parental attachment, parental control, the school social bond and antisocial values have a direct effect on low self-control (impulsivity and aggression). The data are drawn from a sample of young adolescents in Antwerp, Belgium (N = 2,486). The results show that parental control, parental attachment and the school social bond have direct effects on individual differences in low self-control, regardless of family structure. These effects are by and large mediated by antisocial values. The results are highly equivalent for boys and girls and are hardly different for both dimensions of low self-control: impulsivity and aggression. Implications for further studies are discussed.

Chapter 6 - Science has begun to illuminate the mechanisms underlying self-control and its phenomenology. One prevalent hypothesis regarding self-directed,'voluntary' action is that of *ideomotor processing* – that both the guidance and knowledge of one's voluntary actions are limited to perceptual-like representations of action outcomes (e. g. , the'image' of one's finger flexing), with the motor programs/events actually responsible for enacting actions being unconscious. To further examine this basic notion empirically, participants performed simple actions (e. g. , sniffing) while introspecting the degree to which they perceived certain body regions to be responsible for the actions. Consistent with ideomotor theory, participants perceived regions (e. g. , the nose) associated with the perceptual consequences of actions (e. g. , sniffing) to be more responsible for the actions than regions (e. g. , chest/torso) actually generating the action. The authors then examined participants' lay intuitions about perceptual consequences. In addition to supporting ideomotor theory, these findings unveil lay intuitions about the nature of action, perception, and self-control.

Chapter 7 - Self-control or self-management (Kanfer, 1970; Mezo, 2009) is composed of three interdependent constructs: self-monitoring (SM), self-evaluating (SE), and self-reinforcing (SR). To date, a self-management model for anxiety does not exist. Forty-five undergraduate students completed the

Self-Control and Self-Management Scale (SCMS; Mezo, 2009), three measures of social anxiety, and a social desirability measure. As predicted, SM, SE and total SCMS scores negatively correlated with the social anxiety measures. Using a diagnostically valid cutoff score, the participants were divided into low and high anxiety groups. Independent t-tests revealed that the high anxiety group had significant deficits in overall self-management, and significant deficits in SE relative to the low anxiety group. The role of these results in the development of a self- management model for anxiety, along with limitations and possibilities for future research, are discussed.

Chapter 8 - A form of self-control, mental control is essential for children to maintain focus in the classroom and not be distracted by irrelevant stimuli or thoughts. In adults, mental control can backfire, as in the case of *ironic processing*, in which one is more likely to think about something (e. g. , white bears) when instructed to not think about that thing. An interesting finding is that, though children (ages 7-9) can be easily distracted and experience undesired thoughts, they are not susceptible to ironic processing, making them an excellent population in which to study the benefits of increased mental control through external cues. The authors replicated the finding that children are immune from ironic processing, and provide evidence that external cues can increase children's mental control and can diminish their undesired thoughts. This finding begins to illuminate the complex liaisons among attention, set, self-control, and the development of the kinds of executive processes associated with prefrontal cortex.

In: Psychology of Self-Control
Editors: A. Durante, et. al

ISBN: 978-1-61470-881-0
© 2012 Nova Science Publishers, Inc.

Chapter 1

ON YOUNG WOMEN BECOMING SEXUALLY RESOURCEFUL: A PILOT STUDY

Deborah J. Kennett, Terry P. Humphreys and Petrina A. Calder*

Department of Psychology
Trent University
1600 West Bank Drive
Peterborough, ON, Canada

Abstract

It has been shown that highly sexually resourceful women utilize a variety of self-regulatory strategies to deal with unwanted sexual advances that do not involve coercion or sexual assault. What is less understood, however, is how women acquire this skill repertoire. A concurrent mixed-methods approach was used to help unfold this phenomenon. After completing inventories assessing general and sexual resourcefulness skills, nine women were interviewed about their sexual socialization experiences. Four young women, representing the four extreme combinations of scores on these inventories, were first subjected to constant comparative analysis. The substantive model of sexual resourcefulness that emerged from this analysis was further supported by

---

* E-mail address: dkennett@trentu. ca

three additional young cases. The substantive model illustrates that the mass media and peers are influential factors that together have a large impact on women's beliefs about relationships, beauty and body image. Women high in sexual resourcefulness did not subscribe to the values portrayed in the media and also said that their friends outright rejected the messages it conveyed. In sharp contrast, women low in sexual resourcefulness, along with their peer group, were immersed with how they looked and presented themselves in sexual situations, incessantly making comparisons with characters they identified with in the media. Implications for parents and sexual health educators are discussed. Based on the narrative of another two older women, we also describe why for some the development of sexual resourcefulness may come later in life.

Keywords: Resourcefulness, sexual socialization, script theory, self-control, body image.

INTRODUCTION

Voluntarily giving-in to unwanted sexual activity that does not involve physical or psychological force is a common, if not normative, occurrence for young women. In fact, numerous studies using a variety of methods find that approximately 50% of young women report having consented to unwanted sex (Sprecher, Hatfield, Cortese, Potapova, & Levitskaya, 1994; O'Sullivan & Allgeier, 1998; Houts, 2005; Meston & Buss, 2007). Limited research, however, has explored the protective factors equipping young women to best handle these situations.

Pioneering a new area of sexual behavior research, Kennett, Humphreys and Patchell (2009) were the first to examine situations involving sexual decision making and the ways that women handle unwanted sexual activity. In this study, they developed and validated a scale to measure sexual resourcefulness, which is characterized as the ability to employ self-control strategies in unwanted sexual situations. Highly sexually resourceful women, for example, will walk away from or employ other techniques in sexual situations that get out of control or are unwanted. The sexual resourcefulness construct is based on Rosenbaum's (1990) learned resourcefulness - the self-regulatory skills needed to handle everyday life challenges. Kennett et al. (2009) found that women scoring higher on sexual resourcefulness were better able to act in ways that validated their sexual health, such as being less likely to give in to the pressure of unwanted sex. The means by which women acquire these skills, however, is still unknown. Kennett, et al. (2009) found that variables such as age, number of sexual partners, and duration of relationship were all unrelated to the degree of sexual resourcefulness a woman exhibits. The lack of relationship with these variables motivated us to look elsewhere for the source.

Research on the development of learned resourcefulness skills points to a strong relationship between the degree of resourcefulness exhibited by a child and the characteristics of the child's family, especially those of the mother (Zauszniewski, Chung, Chang, & Krafcik, 2002). The likely influence of family in the development of sexual resourcefulness is also supported by research in sexual socialization (Fingerson, 2005). However, family is only one of three commonly cited variables that influence sexual socialization. Peers and the media also play a significant role in determining the sexual attitudes and behaviors of young women (Henry, Schoeny, Deptula & Slavick, 2007; L'Engle, Brown, & Kenneavy, 2006; Tolman & McCelland, 2011). With sexual health information being provided in school curricula, it is also possible that skills are learned in the course of formal instruction.

The purpose of the present study was to delineate the socialization process by which young women acquire their repertoire of sexual resourcefulness skills, attitudes and behaviors. Sexual script theory (Simon & Gagnon, 1986) would likely postulate that cultural messages, combined with individual wants and needs and context, create unique sexual resourcefulness "toolkits" of varying quality. Given that cultural messages come from many sources and are not uniform, a mixed methods design was chosen as the best approach to clarify our understanding of this process. After measuring both one's general repertoire of learned resourcefulness using Rosenbaum's Self-Control Schedule (SCS) and sexual resourcefulness skills using Kennett et al.'s SRS (2009), a small group of young women scoring very high or low on these dimensions were interviewed about their sexual socialization experiences, including the conversations they had with parents and peers, their media exposure and formal education. With the rich data interviews can provide, distinct patterns of socialization might emerge that distinguish women who are highly resourceful from those who lack these skills. Thus, the quantitative distinctions of general and sexual resourcefulness skills, understanding of Kennett et al.'s (2009) sexual self-control model and sexual script theory (Simon & Gagnon, 1986) provided the lens through which the qualitative data was analyzed and understood in this exploratory limited sample design.

Sexual Self-Control Model

Kennett et al.'s (2009) model of sexual self-control delineates the factors empowering young women to better handle situations involving unwanted sexual activity. Their model builds on Rosenbaum's (1980, 1990, 2000) basic model of self-control for health behaviors, whereby the key foundational component is general resourcefulness. Highly resourceful individuals use positive self-talk and problem solving strategies, and delay gratification to handle everyday life situations. Studies on health behaviors have examined the role of general learned resourcefulness in the context of weight loss, exercise, and healthy lifestyle (Kennett & Ackerman, 1995; Kennett & Nisbet, 1998; Kennett, Worth & Forbes, 2009), chronic disease management (Kennett, O'Hagan & Cezer, 2008; White, Tata & Burns, 1996; Zauszniewski & Chung, 2001), and smoking cessation (Kennett, Morris & Bangs, 2006), finding that highly resourceful individuals are more successful dealing with negative emotions or pain, breaking bad habits and adhering to medical regimens than their less resourceful counterparts.

Whether an individual uses this repertoire of well learned skills in stressful encounters depends on a number of factors (e. g. , Humphreys & Kennett, 2010; Kennett et al. , 2009). Environmental and physiological factors, and appraisals of self and the situation (i. e. , process regulating cognitions) influence to what extent self-control behaviors are enacted when obstacles to goals are encountered. In the context of sexual self-control, Kennett et al. (2009) assessed to what extent factors such as sexual self-efficacy, reasons for consenting to a partner, past sexual experiences and general resourcefulness influenced a woman's ability to handle unwanted sexual activity. Results indicated that sexual resourcefulness was directly and negatively related to the experience of giving-in to pressure for sex that was unwanted. They also found, as expected, that a higher general repertoire of learned resourcefulness skills predicted a larger repertoire of sexual resourcefulness skills and that, along with higher sexual self-efficacy and fewer reasons for giving-in to pressure to unwanted sexual activity, these factors accounted for almost 60% of the variance in sexual resourcefulness scores.

As mentioned earlier, no significant relationship was observed between sexual resourcefulness and the demographic variables that would intuitively be expected to predict this skill set. Given the basic assumption from Rosenbaum's model (1990, 2000) that these behavior repertoires are learned through life experience, it is important to consider how it is that women acquire sexual resourcefulness.

Acquisition of Learned Resourcefulness

Maternal qualities play a role in a child's acquisition of general learned resourcefulness skills. Zauszniewski et al. (2002), for instance, examined the child (gender, academic performance, thought patterns), maternal (age, hours working/volunteering, daily functioning, learned resourcefulness) and family (number of parents, number of children) predictors of learned resourcefulness in children aged 10-12 years. Only the child's positive thought patterns and maternal resourcefulness positively predicted the child's level of learned resourcefulness. Given the number of hours the mother spent outside the home (either at work or volunteering) was unrelated to the child's degree of learned resourcefulness, they concluded that it is not the quantity but rather the quality of time a mother and child spend together that facilitates the acquisition of learned resourcefulness.

Family variables have also been found to be predictive of learned resourcefulness in adolescences. Türkel and Tezer (2008) had teens aged 14 to 19 complete the Parenting Style Inventory and the Self-Control Schedule (SCS) assessing general learned resourcefulness skills. Based on responses to the Parenting Style Inventory (assessing degree of acceptance/involvement and strictness/supervision) teens' parents were classified as having a parenting style characterized as Authoritative (i. e. , warm but firm), Neglectful, (i. e. , devote little time and energy to their children), Indulgent (i. e. , high in involvement but make few demands and exercise few controls), or Authoritarian (i. e. , concerned with obedience and conformity rather than the child's autonomy). They found that there was no difference in learned resourcefulness between authoritative and indulgent, or between authoritarian and neglectful parenting styles. However, the teens of self-acclaimed authoritative/indulgent parents scored significantly higher in learned resourcefulness than teens of self-acclaimed authoritarian/neglectful parents. These results suggest that the degree of acceptance and involvement of parents is a stronger determinant of learned resourcefulness than is the degree of strictness or supervision.

In addition to the influence of parenting style, research suggests that family functioning as a whole also influences learned resourcefulness in children. Preechawong, Zauszniewski, Heinzer, Musil, Keresmar, and Aswinanonh (2007) studied the relationships between family functioning, self-esteem, asthma severity and learned resourcefulness in children suffering from asthma. Only family functioning was significantly related to learned resourcefulness, indicating that the more a family works well together as a supportive unit the more resourceful the children in that family will be.

Sexual Script Theory

The process of sexual socialization has been conceptualized by Simon and Gagnon (1986, 2003) as being akin to the development of a script that guides social behavior. Scripts, they suggest, occur at three different levels simultaneously: cultural, interpersonal and intrapsychic. *Cultural scripts* represent the collective understanding of appropriate, socially sanctioned behavior and roles within the larger society. They provide individuals with information that guides their social interactions and are largely taken for granted because of its ubiquitous nature (Simon & Gagnon, 1986). Given that we live in a pluralistic society with a significant amount of ambivalence about sexuality, there are competing cultural scripts regarding sexuality and adolescence (Tolman & McCelland, 2011). *Interpersonal scripts* are concerned with the more concrete details of a specific social interaction, and take into consideration the specifics of the people involved (e. g. , family, peers, teacher) and the context (e. g. , home, school, church), in creating a mental guideline of how an interpersonal exchange will unfold. *Intrapsychic scripts* are concerned with the internal wants and needs of the individual (Gagnon, 1990; Laumann & Gagnon, 1995; Simon & Gagnon, 1986, 2003). The three levels of scripting exist in a state of dynamic tension, with interpersonal scripts often representing a compromise between the cultural and intrapsychic scripts (Gagnon, 1990). The success of a script is determined by the other participants in the social exchange and their expectations created by the applicable cultural scenarios. Successful scripts will be repeated, whereas unsuccessful scripts will be discarded or reworked (Gagnon, 1990). Sexual script theory may help us to understand the ways that various socializing forces influence the behavior of young adults.

Sexual Socialization and Education

Just as the literature on learned resourcefulness points to the family as a primary influence, the literature on sexual socialization also supports the notion that a woman's family has a strong influence on the development of sexual behavior patterns. Fingerson (2005), using mother-adolescent pairs, hypothesized that the teens would demonstrate the influence of their mothers' opinions through the number of sexual partners they had, with more liberal maternal opinion predicting greater numbers of teen sexual partners. This hypothesis was not supported. Instead, Fingerson (2005) found that more liberal maternal attitudes toward sex predicted greater likelihood that a teen would report believing that sex should be a part of a romantic relationship, whether they were currently acting on that belief or not. The study also found that more frequent discussions of sex within the dyad was associated with increased number of sexual partners, while, conversely, a strong mother-child bond was associated with a decreased number of sexual partners. Although these results seem contradictory, it's important to note that the quality and content of the sexual discussions was unknown. What is certain is that mothers are a very strong socializing force in their children's lives, as they impart their understanding of cultural scenarios as filtered through their own personal experiences.

Byers, Sears & Weaver (2008) found that the more comfortable the parent was in discussing sexual topics with their children, and the more positive their own experiences were, the more quantity and quality of conversation with their children they were likely to report. However, the researchers also found that even parents who reported feeling knowledgeable about the topics and comfortable with having the discussions, and who highly rated the quality of their communications with their child, usually reported that they only discuss these topics in very general terms. This suggests a likely gap in the sexual knowledge parents impart on their children that will remain incomplete or be filled, for better or worse, by another socializing force such as peers.

The socializing influence of peers in the life of an adolescent crosses many domains, including sex. Numerous studies have supported the notion that the perception of the sexual attitudes and behaviors of one's peer group has a significant impact on individual adolescent's behavior (Hittner & Kennington, 2008; Potard, Courtois, & Rusch, 2008; Shtarkshall, Carmel, Jaffe-Hirschfield, & Woloski-Wruble, 2009). For example, Sharkshall, et al. (2009) found that the perception of the proportion of peers practicing intercourse was the best predictor of coitus initiation. Hittner and Kennington (2008) found that exaggerated perceptions of peer HIV-risky sexual behavior predicted college students' personal HIV-risky sexual behavior for both males and females. In addition, Henry et al. (2007) found that students reporting participation in sex without condoms were significantly more likely to have also reported the belief that their friends do the same. They also found that the perception of peer attitudes about the "costs" associated with sex were positively related to the attitudes the students themselves reported and negatively related to the likelihood of participating in sex without condoms. It would seem that the influence of peers in the sexual socialization process is a double edged sword. Friends have the potential to have either a positive or negative influence on the sexual attitudes and behaviors one exhibits. The way that a person's friends behave, but more importantly the perception of them, convey the cultural scripts that inform a person's own interpersonal script for behavior.

The sexual content in the mass media is also predictive of sexual behaviors and cognitions in young women. L'Engle et al. (2006), in their study, used a questionnaire to determine the average amount of sexual exposure participants consumed through the mass media. They found that increased exposure to sexual content, through their use of various forms of mass media, predicted more intent to engage in sexual activity and more actual engagement in sexual activity by adolescents, beyond the effect from other socializing forces, including family, peers, race and socioeconomic status. Clearly the sexual messages in the media are influencing the perception of social norms and, by extension, the sexual attitudes and behaviors of young women.

In the language of scripting theory (Simon & Gagnon, 1986), the family, peers and the media send very strong and influential messages to adolescents about cultural scripts, with some of the details being incorporated into interpersonal scripts. However, as previously discussed, these influences always exist in tandem with intrapsychic scripting, dictated by personal needs, wants and preferences. Although it can be argued that these personal desires are just internalized cultural norms, it should be noted that not all of the influencing factors in the life of an adolescent are one-way relationships from the outside-in. When it comes to the influence of sexual content in the media, people are not simply passive recipients of a message. The fact that women choose what media they will expose themselves to adds the element of personal preference to the socialization equation. Viewer involvement with sexualized media (e. g, character identification, perceived realism, critical viewing), in comparison to the sheer amount of viewing, has been shown to influence sexual attitudes and expectations in a number of studies (e. g. , Peter & Valkenburg, 2010; Ward, 1999).

Arnett (1995) also describes two negative consequences of the socializing force of the media. The first is that the messages found about sex in the mass media may be in opposition to those instilled by others, such as family and friends. The disparate messages may be more difficult to integrate into a coherent script. The second problem is that the messages about sex in the mass media are sometimes misleading, incomplete, or simply incorrect. Without a solid foundation for information from other sources to check against, the attitudes and behaviors depicted in the media may result in unhealthy socialization.

It is the intent of formal sexual education in the schools to enhance the skill repertoire of young people. Sexual health education, however, is often "left to the discretion of the individual school boards, school administrations and/or teachers - resulting in inconsistency and variation in the topics covered and time allocated to instruction" (Smylie, Maticka-Tyndale & Boyd, 2008, p. 28). A recent review of sexual health in Canadian schools by the Sex Information and Education Council of Canada (SIECCAN, 2009) suggests that most sex education programs are broadly based with predominant focus and outcome analyses on STDs, unwanted pregnancy and condom use, rather than on intimacy, relationship development and critical skills. Connell's (2005) discourse analysis of the sex education curriculum found that the curricula place emphasis on abstinence, highlighting the negative consequences associated with any sexual activity. Connell (2005) contends that such a message fails to socialize girls to consider a broader range of sexual scenarios and does not provide them with the skills necessary to successfully negotiate any scenario, including one where they may want to say "yes". The very limited range of acceptable sexual behaviors, fail to engage teens in a way that represents a balanced view of what they are experiencing. This skewed and inconsistent approach to sexual education in North America results in yet another gap in the information available to young women about what healthy sexual behavior might be. Without comprehensive information, the behavioral skill sets that young women develop to enact their interpersonal sexual script are bound to be impoverished.

Goals of the Present Study

The purpose of the present study was to understand how young women come to acquire their sexual resourcefulness skills. It is likely that family, peers, the media, and formal educational experiences all contribute to this process long before a woman's first sexual encounter. However, the quantity and quality of information that is learned from each source, as well as the timing of skills acquisition, is unknown. Through their own words, we wanted to explore how women express the influence of these sources based on their levels of resourcefulness.

Guided by a paradigm of realism (see Greene, Benjamin & Goodyear, 2001), a mixed methods approach was used in order to facilitate triangulation of this phenomenon and utility of the results. We recognized that a strictly quantitative approach that employs a diverse range of scales may increase the amount of variability that can be accounted for in sexual resourcefulness but it will not further our understanding of how the skills are acquired by some and not others. Conversely, to employ a strictly qualitative approach to this research question would mean relinquishing two valuable quantitative tools that has been shown to have tremendous value in predicting health behaviors. Thus, to simply guess a woman's level of general and sexual resourcefulness skills based solely on qualitative information runs the risk of error, especially if she possesses only average skills. We also reasoned that sampling women with mid-range scores would diffuse the salient differences that exist among the four quadrants representing the exceptionally high and low generally and sexually resourceful women – a mid-range scoring group's stories would simply emulate a blend of those described by the four extreme archetypes.

METHOD

Sample

Heterosexual female undergraduate students for this study were recruited from a larger survey study conducted by the first two authors aimed at understanding why young women voluntarily consent to unwanted sexual activity. Of the 330 students who took part in this online survey study, 201 of them (at the time of this study) were still involved in courses where they received bonus credit for their choice of either participating in research or writing reports on empirical papers. Of these 201 students, 24 of them were invited to participate in a 60 to 90 minute interview who exhibited very high or low scores on both the Self-Control Schedule (SCS) and Sexual Resourcefulness Scale (SRS), representing the extreme quartiles of these distributions, with 5 women volunteering. In order to improve the participation rate, 16 further women, some with less extreme SCS scores, were invited to participant in the study, of which 4 women volunteered. A total of 9 students were interviewed. All interviewees had completed the SCS and SRS four to six weeks prior to the interview. Two highly generally resourceful, but moderately sexually resourceful participants were at least 10 years older. Their scripts were used to validate claims made in the discussion. The seven remaining participants were 18 to 20 years old.

Procedure

Interviews were conducted in a quiet and comfortable research lab. Informed consent, approved by the University's Research Ethics Board, was obtained before each interview began. All interviews were digitally recorded and transcribed verbatim, and field notes were taken during and immediately following each interview. Participants received a one hour bonus credit toward their first or second year psychology course. After each interview, the participant was debriefed and provided with a feedback letter that included contact information for counseling services, if needed. The interviewer (third author) remained blind to the quantitative cohort of each participant until after all interviews were completed and transcribed. Participants were not aware of their grouping with respect to general and sexual resourcefulness. All of them completed the interview in its entirety.

Quantitative Measures

Rosenbaum's (1980) Self-Control Schedule (SCS) is widely used in the literature to assess general learned resourcefulness skills. It consists of 36 items, which are rated on a six-point Likert scale ranging from -3 very uncharacteristic of me to +3 very characteristic of me. In the management of their everyday life, individuals are asked to what extent they rely on problem solving strategies (e. g. , "When I am faced with a difficult problem, I approach it in a systematic way"), use positive self statements to cope with stressful situations (e. g. , "When an unpleasant thought is bothering me, I think about something pleasant"), and are able to delay gratification (e. g. , "I prefer to finish a job that I have to do before I start doing things I really like"). Scores can range from -108 to 108, with mean scores for student populations typically around 24 and with a standard deviation of 25 (e. g. , Rosenbaum, 1980). Higher scores reflect greater levels of general learned resourcefulness skills. The reliability and the validity of the SCS have been well established and documented, with test re-test and internal consistency coefficients exceeding . 80 (e. g. , Rosenbaum, 1980, 1990).

The level of sexual resourcefulness was measured using Kennett et al.'s (2009) 19-item Sexual Resourcefulness Scale (SRS). Items reflect behaviors and self-instructions that can be implemented immediately to handle unwanted sexual advances or actions that are planned in advance (e. g. , *I always have a back up plan for when I am faced with unwanted sexual advances/activity that get out of control*; *Although I feel bad about hurting my partner's feelings, I let him know when I am uncomfortable with a sexual situation*). Items are rated on a six-point Likert scale, with 1 being "least characteristic of me", to 6 being "most characteristic of me". Higher total scores reflect higher use of sexual self-control strategies, and can range from 19 to 104, with an average total score of 80. 51 (SD = 18. 36). Internal consistency of this scale is . 91 (Humphreys & Kennett, 2010; Kennett et. al, 2009), and test-retest reliability is . 78 (Humphreys & Kennett, 2011).

Qualitative Data-Collection

A semi-structured interview protocol, consisting of ten open-ended questions along with follow-up probes, was used to inquire about the sexual socialization and education experiences of the participants. Given the literature on sexual socialization and on the acquisition of learned resourcefulness both suggest a strong influence of maternal and family characteristics, the interview protocol was designed to ask about these factors specifically (e. g. , *When you were growing up, tell me the type of things that you were comfortable with confiding in your parents/mother/father*). We also asked questions about the media (e. g. , *In general what kind of T. V. shows do you like to watch? What kind of movies? What kind of music videos? Describe how these media reflect real life and intimate relationships?*), and about their sex education in school (e. g. , *Describe your experience with sexual education in school? What do you remember learning? How were these lessons helpful in your personal experiences?*).

Design and Analysis

The current study employed a concurrent mixed methods design (Creswell, 2003), whereby qualitative and quantitative data were analyzed together, for the purposes of enhancement, utility, triangulation and sampling (see Bryman, 2006, for description of these purposes). The interview transcripts were subjected to constant comparison, and at each level of analysis we referred back to the original transcript in order to verify that our interpretations were true to the context provided in the narrative. Information was always interpreted within the context of other information provided during each interview and compared to that provided by others within the same quantitative cohort (when it was applicable) and across cohorts. The level of abstraction in the themes that emerged was kept close to the data by extensive use of verbatim quotes. Analysis was verified through peer debriefing, as all authors met frequently to discuss the cases and the emergent themes and model. During these discussions of the data, we reached the same interpretation of the narratives providing a high degree of auditability. Understanding of the data was further verified through constant revisiting of the source data, and through triangulation with the framework of script theory and the model of learned resourcefulness.

RESULTS

Quantitative features of the original sample

For the original sample ($N = 330$), scores on the SCS ranged from -71 to 85 and the scores on the SRS ranged from 40 to 109, with scores of both distributions being normally distributed. Concerning the upper and lower quartiles, 25% of the sample had SCS scores greater than 29 and lower than -5 points. For the SRS, 25% of the sample had scores greater than 95 and lower than 73 points. The correlation between the SCS and SRS was relatively low but significant, $r(328) = .38, p < .001$. So it was not surprising that, for our sub-sample of 201 students, it was more common to find extremely highly resourceful women to also score extremely high in sexual resourcefulness ($N = 26$; 54%) and extremely low resourceful women to also score extremely low in sexual resourcefulness ($N = 24$; 46%). In contrast, there were only 3 extremely low SCS/high SRS (6%) and 3 extremely high SCS/low SRS (6%) women to select from in these quartiles. Equally noteworthy, only 8.4% of our moderately low SCS women and only 5% of our moderately high SCS women were found to be extremely high in sexual resourcefulness, suggesting that sexual resourcefulness is a skill repertoire that develops later in life for adolescent women depending on their level of general resourcefulness skills.

Participants in our study

The seven participants considered in this analysis were categorized according to their SCS and SRS scores. Due to the fact that the high SCS/high SRS and low SCS/high SRS categories were each represented by only a single participant, and two of the participants had only moderately high SCS scores but extremely low SRS scores, an exploratory qualitative analysis with a limited sample was adopted. The initial analysis, thus, reflected four participants having either the most extremely high SCS (36 or greater)/ SRS (96 or greater) or the most extremely low SCS (-4 or lower)/SRS (72 or lower) scores, representing the upper and lower quadrants of the SCS and SRS distributions. A summary of these participants' scores are shown in Table 1.

Table 1. The SCS and SRS scores of the four archetypes used in the initial phase of the analysis

		General Resourcefulness (SCS)	
		High	Low
Sexual Resourcefulness	High	SCS/SRS = 49/107	SCS/SRS = -38/105
(SRS)	Low	SCS/SRS = 36/68	SCS/SRS = -35/64

Comparative Analysis

Using a constant comparative analysis approach, two similarities were observed across all four cases/archetypes. First, the experiences of formal sexual education in school curriculum were virtually uniform. All four participants noted learning the same information, in the same grade, and commented that lessons were approached from a biological rather than a practical stance. In fact, the narratives of sexual education experiences across all nine interviews were so similar in content that they are almost interchangeable. The second similarity observed was the lack of involvement by fathers in the sexual socialization of these women. Although fathers were noted as background figures in the narratives, none of the participants indicated a willingness to confide in her father, and some indicated actively avoiding discussion of sex, sexuality, and intimate relationships with him.

Table 2. Selected quotes from the archetypes depicting the themes

High SCS – High SRS (HH) Archetype

Internalization of Values

I don't think [the media reflects real life and intimate relationships] at all. I think they're quite harmful actually, sometimes […] they don't even portray the beauty of relationships…They're actually covering what is the real beauty of it. (p. 17, 6-10)

Analysis of the most extreme four archetypes also resulted in the identification of five distinct but related themes: Internalization of Values, Support and Validation, Information Seeking, Reflection and Synthesis, and Perspectives of Others. Selected quotes from these cases depicting the themes are presented in Table 2, providing transparency to our analysis.

Support and Validation

When I talked to my brother [about a troubling sexual incident] [...] he made me feel like, okay, I've been in to something bad, I did something stupid and, in some ways but I got out of it and I learned something from it. (p. 13, 13-15)

Information Seeking

[Sex] was a very ambiguous thing for me growing up. [...] And my mother never really talked about it, [...] watching a documentary of the sperm and the egg and suddenly it made sense. And, but I discovered it by myself. (p. 5-6, 20-2)

Reflection and Synthesis

[...] Friendships determine a lot of who you are, and they mold you a lot. And, just as you mold them [...] and because of that influence, because of being exposed to these people, my idea of my sexual life in general get shaped and re-shaped through them. And it's like [...] these ideas are evolving with us. (p. 19, 7-11)

Perspective of Others

[My conversations with my brother are] pretty broad. [...] We also talk about relationships and how we feel. I think we cover many sides of our lives. (p. 4, 16-19)

Low SCS – Low SRS (LL) Archetype

Internalization of Values

I love Britney Spears and Christina Aguillera and I loved the Backstreet Boys. And I've grown... and I watched those videos. And I honestly think that's part of my body image is I grew up watching, you know, God love her but beautiful skinny Britney Spears, and that put a lot of pressure on me. (p. 11, 12-15)

Support and Validation

By the time I started in sexual situations I had kind of turned more inwards. That's when I started sharing less with my mom. [...] I don't know, I think I felt maybe like I was going to let her down or something like that. That's when [...] Google became a good friend. And I would share with friends, but I felt like I was doing things, or kind of ahead of the game. (p. 8-9, 21-4)

Information Seeking

I feel like [formal sex education] came too late. I mean, kids start doing silly things when they're younger and younger. [...] like we should have known how to put a condom on a banana or something by grade 8 at least. (p. 7, 1-4)

Reflection and Synthesis

The Internet and magazines and through friends, I've become I feel a more powerful woman. And I think that's reflected in the fact that I used to read the gossip magazines and I liked to turn on the Britney Spears videos [...] that's part of my personal growth that I've turned toward [...] I mean, nothing is more powerful than Buffy the Vampire Slayer who can beat up everything! She kicks butt. (p. 13, 15-22)

Perspective of Others

[Perspective of others was limited. This was the only excerpt we could find] When I was 11 or 12, my mom started talking about the period-thing. I guess in her childhood that had crept up on her and no one had explained it and she was terrified and she didn't want that to happen to me. (p. 3, 6-10)

Low SCS – High SRS (LH) Archetype

Internalization of Values

The media is sensationalized, stupid and it's just, everything's, improbable and not helpful at all. (p. 12, 14-15)

Support and Validation

It's just all girls [on a particular social networking website], so it's, a lot of them feel really comfortable and I feel comfortable talking, since I don't really know them. But I know them through what they've said. (p. 9, 2-4)

Information Seeking

Sex Ed. [...] gave the basics [...] but friends, like, put it into practice and you learn from them, and you share information. It's [...]'This did this and I didn't like it' or'So-and-so did this and I wasn't really comfortable with it' or'So-and-so did that and it was really cool.' (p. 12, 3-7)

Reflection and Synthesis

[…] And if I didn't like [a sexual advance] I would say'Okay, you know, I don't like that' and they would […] stop and they wouldn't do it again. (p. 6, 10-15)

Perspective of Others

[None - She does not elaborate on others' opinions, distinguish any one particular friend, or express empathy for another.]

High SCS – Low SRS (HL) Archetype

Internalization of Values

With my guy friends here we had a big conversation about what guys look for in girls and stuff…Body image in the media and everything, you're told to look a certain way and if you don't look like this then you won't be attractive to other people. (HL, p. 6, 13-20)

Support and Validation

I've been going through personal, kind of self-confidence issues, and my friends are helping me out with that too, supporting me. But it's really really hard. (p. 7, 1-3)

Information Seeking

I remember actually there was one [website] growing up called gurl. com and everybody kind of knew it and you'd just go there and look at whatever you wanted. […] (p. 12, 12-16) I liked the idea that there was this discussion board with people your age too. […] (p. 12, 20-22) […] It's just nice to know that somebody else is as lost as you, […] and that was one of my questions too […] (p. 13, 3-7)

Reflection and Synthesis

I'll see other girls around, just in general, and they have like countless boyfriends […] And so I feel sometimes like what am I doing wrong? So I try to fix it with my appearance. […] I will not go to lecture without having my full face done up, nothing. Cause I'm just too self-conscious. I feel like everybody will stare at me if I don't look like this [with full make-up, hair styled, manicure, and stylish dress]. (p. 7, 6-13)

Perspective of Others

My mom she wasn't, I don't want to say she never went out, but she was the kind of person that like stayed in, study study study, […]. And my dad too, he was really really book smart. And so for me, when we talk about going to parties and stuff, they just don't understand because they were never, they didn't do that. (p. 1, 16-20)

Internalization of Values

Participants were cognizant that influences outside themselves affected their self-esteem and views about body image, as well as their sexual attitudes and behaviors, whether the source of the value judgment was a parent, peer group or the mass media. Some of these messages about values were rejected by the participants, while others were adopted and internalized as their own.

In particular, the influence of ideals in the mass media clearly differentiated the low SRS participants from the high SRS participants. Both of the low SRS participants had a strong identification with the media. Not only did they describe consuming more media than the high SRS participants, but they also expressed identification with the characters they viewed, with both low SRS participants believing that these images were highly idealized versions of real life. Moreover, both low SRS participants said that the media greatly shaped the ideals that they were striving to achieve regarding beauty and relationships. As a result of failing to meet these ideals, they described their struggles with low self-esteem and body image issues.

Conversely, the high SRS participants outright rejected the media. In short, they did not identify with any of the characters portrayed in the media, believing that the media did not reflect real life, even in an idealized form.

Support and Validation

All of the participants noted at least one person in their current lives, or in the past, who was a source of emotional support. Whether the supporting person was a family member or a friend and whether the participant had only one or many supporters, varied across these cases. However, the importance of having someone to rely on for emotional needs was articulated by all four archetypes.

Interestingly, it was the low SCS participants who expressed having very close relationships with their mothers. These women described their mothers as being very open with them, emotionally supportive and someone whom they could confide in about many issues in their lives, except for sexual experiences. In contrast, the high SCS participants had a great deal of love and affection for their mothers but expressed that their mothers could not be a confidant. They attributed this distance to generational differences and the fact that their mothers could not understand or support their choices.

The quality of peer support also varied among the four archetypes. The two low SRS participants indicated that they had supportive peers now, but that at the time they were becoming sexually active their friends were unable to be supportive or understand their point of view due to lack of experience. The two high SRS participants, in contrast, were well supported, although the source of the support was different in each case. The low SCS/high SRS (LH) case relied a lot on her peers, and commented that they were also more experienced than she was. The high SCS/high SRS (HH) case did not turn to her friends for support at all, but rather to her older brother, a medical doctor, whom she emulated.

Expressions of feeling validated were also present in all four cases, but manifested in very different ways. The HH case sought out peers with similar values, and had a positive intimate relationship that helped her to appreciate her unique beauty. She also found validation through her academic courses and by connecting her experiences and perspectives with those expressed by others publicly, in her seminars. The high SCS/low SRS (HL) and LH participants sought validation mainly from their peer groups. The HL participant expressed mixed feelings, on the one hand identifying strongly with her peers, but on the other hand constantly comparing herself to those around her, feeling that she often did not measure up. The LH participant felt validated by her peers all along, both online and in person, and through a positive intimate relationship. The low SCS/low SRS (LL) case clearly struggled with finding validation, but noted that her worth and esteem came from her attractiveness to the opposite sex.

Information Seeking

When it came to learning about sex, not all of the desired information was either given by a parent or included in formal sex education. In order to close gaps in their knowledge, participants engaged in varying degrees of information seeking behavior. Even though the sources used differed, and the type of information sought varied, all participants endeavored to educate, inform, and prepare themselves for handling sexual situations.

The HH case did not engage in very much information seeking. Rather, because her confidant was an older sibling and medical doctor, she felt that she was able to access all the information she needed through him. The LH participant said that her peer group openly shared a great deal of practical information and situation specific strategies, both in person and through an online social networking site.

As indicated earlier, both of the low SRS participants indicated that their peers were not a source of information at the time they became sexually active, due to their friends' lack of experience and, in one case, the girl's shyness in discussing the topic. Instead, both low SRS participants accessed the same website as their primary source of information about sex. This website, marketed to young women, provides some information about sex, but also includes articles about fashion and movies, and includes games and polls. The HL participant used the website primarily for the discussion board, where she could talk openly with other girls her age about the sexual questions she had. The LL participant, on the other hand, did not distinguish how she used the site and referenced the entertainment content as much as the informative content. She also began reading Cosmopolitan magazine at a very young age specifically to acquire information about sex and fashion.

Reflection and Synthesis

The two highly generally resourceful cases (HH and HL) engaged in a great deal of evaluation, whereas the two low SCS cases (LL and LH) exhibited limited amounts of reflection. The HH participant reflected a great deal on what she had learned and the reasons for the choices she had made or opinions she expressed. In particular, she talked at length about the role of the media in society and was critical of the often alienating values and lifestyles it portrays. She also expressed awareness of the power of peers to influence one's sexual attitudes and behaviors.

The HL participant was also very reflective in her interview and often cited the reasons for her opinions and support for them. Also similar to the HH participant, the HL case was aware that the power of peers could have both a positive and negative influence on one's thoughts and actions regarding sexuality and relationships. She also felt a great deal of pressure from both her social group and the media to conform to the ideals portrayed in the mainstream. Even though she recognized the negative effect these pressures were having on her body image and self-esteem, she did not reject them. This participant instead expressed gratitude for her peers because they had helped her to find a balance between the strict values of her parents and the social life she desired.

Unlike the two high SCS archetypes, the low SCS participants engaged in very little reflection during their interviews. Each case, though, did express instances where she had synthesized information drawn from different areas of her life. The LH participant detailed how, when she is in a new situation with a sexual partner, she felt comfortable with discovering her own behavioral strategies via trial and error, while keeping in mind the experiences and information shared previously with her peers. The fact that she is confident doing so, and that she provided an example of an occasion where she asserted her right to say no to a partner who was doing something that made her uncomfortable, suggests that she had successfully integrated not just the information and strategies, but also the support and validation messages of her self-worth.

The LL participant expressed her desire and past efforts to improve her self-concept, especially with regard to her body image. She was not skilled, however, at distinguishing information from entertainment in the sources she referenced. Although she did reflect briefly on the negative influence of the mass media in her life, she came to the faulty conclusion that she had simply been referencing the wrong media.

Perspectives of Others

In the course of their narrative, all participants mentioned the people who currently play a role in their lives or who had been a part of their life in the past. The high SCS participants described these supporting players with rich detail. Both of these women expressed the point of view of their parents, and explained how these opinions differed from their own. Furthermore, while they do not share their values, the high SCS women do express empathy for their mothers' perspective and an understanding of how that perspective leads to each mother's feelings about her daughter's choices. Conversely, the low SCS participants spoke of the people in their lives only in terms of the role the person filled, such as "friend" or "mother". They did not articulate any perspective other than their own throughout their interviews. These narratives were more self-focused in tone.

Substantive Model of Sexual Resourcefulness

From this analysis, a substantive model emerged, which is graphically illustrated in Figure 1. Particular attention was given to the distinctions between cases of high and low sexual resourcefulness.

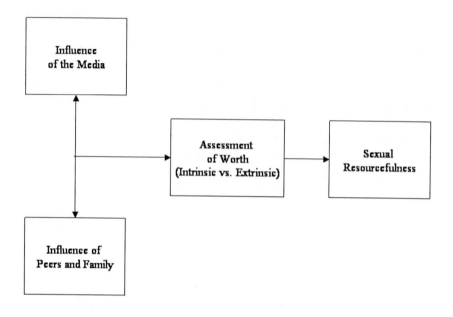

Figure 1. Substantive model reflecting the acquisition of sexual resourcefulness.

Influence of the Media

The role of the media in the lives of young women is undeniable. All four women remarked that they use various forms of media, and three of the four cases said that they felt the beauty ideals portrayed in the media had a negative affect on their body-image. However, the degree to which women internalize the media's ideals differed markedly between high and low sexually resourceful women. For the high SRS women, the media does not embody the ideals they personally subscribe to. They recognize that the media portrays a false and limiting version of reality, and they do not look to the media for examples, information or ideals. Low SRS cases, on the other hand, look to the mass media as demonstrating the ideals for beauty, sexuality, and intimate relationships. These women are not deluded, and recognize that the vision the media portrays is not entirely congruent with reality. But rather than seeing it as false, the low SRS women see it as an idealized version of reality. For these women, the media does serve as an example for how women should look, feel, and behave.

Influence of Peers and Family

Having access to support and information, which enables a young woman to confide and learn from her experiences, is very important in the development of sexual resourcefulness. High SRS women are closer to their peers and have more in depth conversations about sex with them. They also have a positive and secure source of emotional support from a family member and have people close to them with whom to share their sexual experiences.

Low SRS women expressed that they lack quality peer support and information regarding sex, and both of the participants turned to the internet to try to fill the gap. However, each woman used this tool in a different way, with the HL participant seeking out support through online peer communities, while the LL sought out factual information. In both cases, because they lacked a quality source of support and information in their personal lives, they were unable to discuss their experiences, share their concerns, or have a source from whom to learn situation specific strategies. Family is also not seen as a resource by these women. Though the HL participant respects her mother, she commented numerous times that she would be very unlikely to confide in her mother about sex or go to her for information. Similarly, the LL participant expressed that she stopped confiding in her mother once she became sexually active, despite the fact that she had shared a very close and supportive relationship with her mother up until that point in her life. Whatever the reason, family is not viewed as a source of support or information by the women who are low in sexual resourcefulness.

The Mutual Influence of Media and Peers

As depicted in Figure 1, the influence of the media and peers is reciprocal. It is not possible to say whether young women are first influenced by the media and then seek out peer groups who share their values, or whether it is the peer groups who are influenced by the media and in turn establish the normative expectations for their friends. The truth is likely to be both. Peer group values, nevertheless, clearly differentiate the women who are high in sexual resourcefulness from those low in sexual resourcefulness. The highly sexually resourceful women, for instance, reject the media's values and describe peer groups who are also disengaged from the mainstream media. Whereas, the low sexually resourceful women internalize the media's messages about beauty and intimate relationship ideals and describe peer groups who have also adopted these values.

Intrinsic vs. Extrinsic Assessment of Body Self-Worth

Women who are high in sexual resourcefulness do not internalize the media's impossible beauty standards and have much more inclusive and realistic ideals for beauty, sex, and relationships. In short, they are accepting of their own appearance, body image, and sexual experiences. These assessments are also validated by their peers, who share the same values as these young women. Given their beliefs about beauty come from within, these women are empowered to employ their sexual resourcefulness skills to act in their own self-interest and preserve their sexual rights.

In contrast, the low sexually resourceful women are extrinsic about their body self-worth. By internalizing the media's standards for beauty, sex, and relationships, these women and their peers have created a situation where they will almost always fall short of their ideals. The detrimental effects of the media on self-esteem and body image were clearly articulated in both of the low SRS cases. When a woman assesses her beauty and body image based on extrinsic factors, she is disempowered to act in sexually resourceful ways. It is possible that low SRS women do not even conceive of resourceful behaviors as within their realm of possible choices. And even if such a woman did want to behave resourcefully in a sexual situation, it is unlikely that she will have learned the necessary skills and strategies from her peer group. The quality of information accessed by women low in SRS, either through the internet or from peers, is impoverished because they seek information from media sources, such as Cosmopolitan magazine and reality shows on TV.

Additional Support for Substantive Model

Three additional cases were similar in age to the women depicted in the four archetypes and provide further support for the proposed substantive model. Two of these women scored moderately high in general resourcefulness and extremely low in sexual resourcefulness (28/66 and 26/59, i. e. , ML). Given Rosenbaum (1980) and others (e. g. Kennett et al. , 2006) report that the typical mean of the SCS measure for student populations is around 24, these two women, having SCS scores of 26 and 28, are considered moderate rather than extremely high in general resourcefulness. The third woman's scores (-8/65, i. e. , LL) classify her as being extremely low in general as well as sexual resourcefulness. Even though the SCS scores of these women are less extreme than the four cases previously described, these additional examples all had SRS scores that were similar to two of the archetypes (i. e. , LL and HL cases) and are classified as extremely low on the measure of sexual resourcefulness.

Influence of the Media

Although most women are influenced in some way by the images and ideals of the mass media, women who are low in sexual resourcefulness are more likely to have internalized these ideals as their own. Each of the three additional low sexually resourceful women discussed the way that they emulate the media in their own life. For example, one woman said "Everyone does strive to be perfect, like from magazines to shows, so like The Hills and everything. [...]. And you're just like, "Wow, what do they use?" (28/66, p. 10, 13-17). Although they recognize that the images portrayed in the media are a fantasy, these low sexually resourceful women view the images as idealized versions of reality, rather than as inaccuracies.

The reason that I love watching [reality TV shows] is that there's so many different people. [...] But it's never to the extreme that the music videos or movies do it. So, they're definitely more realistic. (26/59, p. 11, 15-20)

The influence of the mass media in the lives of low sexually resourceful women is highly conspicuous in their narratives. The unrealistic ideals for beauty, intimate relationships, and feminine behavior are viewed as true and worthy goals for these women to follow.

Influence of Family and Peers

For women low in sexual resourcefulness, family and peers tended not to be a positive resource in regard to their sexual lives. Peers in particular were unhelpful, serving as cautionary tales for these three women rather than positive or knowledgeable role models. Each woman commented on observing the mistakes of friends and that these events were surprising.

I actually know people who have gotten STDs and you're like, "Whoa! That actually happened!" (28/66, p. 7, 18-19).

These women also expressed a hesitancy to confide about their sexual lives with peers.

[...] But as I got older I realized that I didn't have to confide in my friends as much. [...] It's just kind of between you and your partner. (-8/59, p. 2, 13-16).

These women also noted that friends were a poor source for advice or information because they lacked experience.

When you're getting advice from somebody who hadn't been through it, like how are you telling me what to do when you've never been through it? (-8/65, p. 16, 13-14).

The influence of family in the sexual socialization of two of these women is also notably absent. For one of the ML participants (26/59), sex was never discussed in her household and her parents slept in separate rooms. Everything she learned about sex, including menstruation, was taught by her older sister who she noted had learned from Cosmopolitan magazine. Her parents were also not emotionally supportive and she said of their relationship "I hated not being able to go and talk to my parents. " (26/59, p. 16, 21) The LL participant (-8/65) was simply told by her mother to be smart and safe, but never elaborated on exactly what she meant by either smart or safe behavior. However, this participant did note that her mother was a source of emotional support for her when it came to matters other than sex. The third woman (28/66) represents an anomaly in regard to the influence of family. She expressed having a very open relationship with her mother, who was willing to discuss sex in specific detail. However, during the course of the interview this participant indicated that if she had an important situation to handle, such as becoming accidentally pregnant, that her mother would be the last person to tell and only because she would feel guilty for withholding the information.

Of these three additional cases, only one participant sought additional information or support from outside sources. One of the ML women (26/59) expressed that she had visited the health unit and made use of an online support site, to address very specific situational needs.

Mutual influence of Peers and the Media

These women, who are low in sexual resourcefulness, have internalized the ideals of the mass media and also tend to have peer groups who share these values. This is best articulated by one ML participant in particular (28/66). She commented that her "friends will base their life around TV shows. " (28/66, p. 22, 10-11) Furthermore, she sees her life as being akin to the kinds of melodramas portrayed on TV.

I think The Hills is a prime example of how people act, in their relationships. Like, my girlfriends could have our own reality TV show, like with the drama that goes on between girls and guys. [...] (28/66, p. 25, 15-18).

Intrinsic vs. Extrinsic Assessment of Body Self-Worth

Based on the proposed substantive model, we would expect women who are low in sexual resourcefulness to assess their own beauty and body image based on extrinsic measures, such as the media's standard for beauty. This was certainly emulated by these three women. Field notes indicate that each of these women arrived at the interview in stylish dress, with full make-up, hair-styling, and manicures, as did our two archetypes scoring low in sexual resourcefulness that were described earlier. One participant stated that how she presents herself is very intentional.

Regardless of who you are, [the media] still influences you. Like, [...] you want to portray an image no matter if it's positive or negative, [...] in what you wear, and what you do, and how you act. (28/66, p. 25, 5-8).

Despite intentional choices to convey a certain beauty standard, all three women expressed during their interviews the feeling that their self-esteem and body image had decreased with age and experience. For example, one person said "I definitely find myself more self-conscious [about my body] now than I was [when I first became sexually active]" (26/59, p. 5, 5-6).

Rather than learning to appreciate their bodies through experience and maturity, these women have instead become further saturated with the media's ideals over time. One woman also articulated that meeting the ideals seen in the media bestows status on a woman.

I think that people mimic the celebrities, [...] You see some celebrity wearing expensive jeans and then you wear expensive jeans. It's like, a status thing. (28/66, p. 24, 16-19).

DISCUSSION

The highly generally resourceful participants exhibited differences from their less generally resourceful counterparts that are similar to those that have been detailed in other mixed methods research using the SCS (e. g. , Kennett, O'Hagen & Cezer, 2008). Distinctions include that people high in general resourcefulness demonstrate more reflection on their experiences, more consideration of alternate points of view, and greater synthesis of information in their narratives.

Being generally resourceful, however, does not necessarily lead to high levels of sexual resourcefulness. Even though it was far more likely for women in our original sub-sample (N = 201) to either score in the upper quartile on both the SCS and SRS or in the lower quartile on both the SCS and SRS, many of the moderately generally resourceful women in this sample scored extremely low in sexual resourcefulness. As clearly portrayed by the LH archetype, sexual resourcefulness is a very domain specific skill set, and is influenced by the cultural scenarios one accepts. For instance, our highly sexually resourceful women believed beauty came from within, and not from modeling the look of women and types of relationships seen in the media. Nonetheless, the combination of high general and sexual resourcefulness provided a perspective that was unique in this study. High levels of general resourcefulness, combined with high domain specific resourcefulness, allow one to reach a deeper level of sexual actualization. The HH participant was the only one to discuss the importance of meaning and emotion in intimate relationships, and she articulated a greater depth of appreciation for the beauty of human relationships and acceptance of the imperfections inherent in them. This sophisticated rhetoric about intimacy was not evident in any of the other quantitative cohorts.

Although Rosenbaum's Model of Self-Control Behavior (1990) helped us to understand the complex and dynamic factors that contribute to the expression of sexual resourcefulness skills, it was Script Theory (Simon & Gagnon, 1986) especially during the analysis phase that came to life, as the narratives of the participants illustrated the theory in action. The extent to which intrapsychic scripts are informed by the cultural scenarios reflected in the media is different for high and low sexually resourceful women. Women high in sexual resourcefulness have internalized the message from a variety of other sources (e. g. , peers, postsecondary education) that they have intrinsic worth and unique beauty, and, thus, their intrapsychic script about their sexual needs and preferences have extensively filtered the cultural norms displayed in the media. For the HH archetype, her main intrapsychic script was securing an intimate and meaningful relationship, whereas for the LH archetype, her prominent intrapsychic script was being in total control when sexually uncomfortable with her partner. Conversely, women low in sexual resourcefulness subscribe to the extrinsic, stereotyped ideals that are portrayed in media regarding beauty, relationships and sex, and have internalized these cultural scenarios as their own intrapsychic scripts.

Interpersonal scripts are concerned with the more concrete details of a given social interaction, and are informed by cultural and intrapsychic scripts. The participants noted that peers were the source they first turn to for information about sexual specific sexual strategies. However, the quality of information provided varied dramatically and clearly distinguished between women who were high versus low in sexual resourcefulness. Women high in sexual resourcefulness turned to trusted peers who shared and validated their values. Women low in sexual resourcefulness also turned to trusted peers, but their peer groups, unlike for the highly sexually resourceful women, were unable to provide them with the needed concrete details to formulate an effective script for interpersonal, sexual, encounters.

The fact that parents seem to play a very small role in the development of this domain specific resourcefulness is due, at least in part, to the fact that there is, as Byers' et al. (2006) found, a communication gap between parents and their daughters about sex. In our interviews, fathers were barely mentioned and when they were it was to simply say that they have no role in this aspect of their daughter's life. This has been supported recently by Hutchinson and Cederbaum (2011) who found that most daughters reported receiving very little sexual information from their families. Mothers, though they often feature prominently in the narratives of these young women, provided more general emotional support and were not a source of information about practical strategies in sexual situations.

Sexual education classes, another possible source of information for young women, were unanimously panned by the participants in this study. Despite the fact that they experienced sexual education in different cities and that some were enrolled in the Catholic school system and others in the public school system, their accounts of these experiences were virtually identical. Participants noted that, with few exceptions, teachers were awkward with the material they were teaching. Perhaps because of this unease, or because it is presented in the same context as other fact-based lessons, the sexual education curriculum is typically taught as theory and fact rather than as practical and applicable life skills.

Students in turn are no more comfortable learning about sex in this context than teachers are with presenting the material. Participants noted that students are inhibited to ask questions for fear of negative judgments from peers. Furthermore, nervous energy in the classroom often resulted in jokes and giggling to diffuse the awkward feelings. The overall sentiment was that the curriculum's approach to sexual education is inadequate and the context it is presented in prohibits class participation. Due to these factors, students don't personally relate to the lessons and they instead rely on peers to figure out how to put knowledge into practice.

Implications for Practice

With our new understanding of the role media plays in the acquisition of sexual resourcefulness skills, there is a great opportunity for both parents and educators to teach girls about the influence of the media in their lives. Although most of us take this influence for granted as adults, children do not realize the manipulations that are employed by the media to encourage consumerism and bias our thinking. As pointed out by Arnett (1995), adolescents make use of the media as a tool to self-socialize, but for some teens this tool inhibits the development of a positive self-image instead of empowering it.

The values portrayed in the media, such as unnatural beauty standards or status being determined by possessions, are detrimental to the development of intrinsic self-worth. For this reason, parents and educators alike need to more openly discuss this influence with girls starting at a very young age. Programs that help to unveil the ways that women's images are manipulated in print advertising may prove to be a valuable resource. The purpose is to help young women become savvy and critical consumers of the media, rather than passive receivers of the message. With a focus on helping young women to feel an intrinsic sense of self-worth, it may be possible to counteract some of the media's influence that is inhibiting the development of sexual resourcefulness.

The biggest challenge for any woman in becoming sexually resourceful is the struggle to subvert the influence of the media and establish peer connections that validate both her rejection of the media's standards and her acceptance of her own unique beauty. However, this is a challenge that many young women don't even realize they are facing. The substantive model described in this paper reflects the fact that all women struggle with the influence of the media in their lives, especially when it comes to body image. Knauss, Paxton and Alsaker (2008), in their quantitative study, discovered that perceived pressure from media predicted body dissatisfaction and internalization of the media body ideal. Clearly the focus of parents and educators, who wish to arm young women with sexual resourcefulness skills, needs to be squarely on helping them to value intrinsic qualities over extrinsic indicators of worth, appreciate conceptions of beauty that fall outside of the norm portrayed in the media and accept their imperfections.

Equally important for parents and sex education classes is to help women realize the meanings and emotions involved in relationships, as our highly generally and sexually resourceful (HH) archetype did. As well, both of our highly sexually resourceful women were not only comfortable with themselves, they also had little difficulty saying no in uncomfortable sexual situations. The practical need and implications of these qualities for all young women is timely given the predominant cultural messages young women are exposed to by the media.

Lastly, parents and teachers need to be cognizant of the timing and tempo of pubertal development and its influence on sexual resourcefulness skills. Research has demonstrated that early development is associated with earlier initiation of sexual intercourse and is a risk factor for body image concerns (Deardorff, Gonzales, Christopher, Roosa, & Millsap, 2005; Miller, Norton, Curtis, Hill, Schvaneveldt, & Young, 1997; Striegel-Moore, McMahon, Biro, Schreiber, Crawford, & Voorhees, 2001). For many of our low sexually resourceful women, they indicated having sex even before sex education classes were introduced into their curricula. We surmise that early pubertal development not only place young girls at higher risk for STDs, and unwanted pregnancies, but also for the establishment of a low generally and low sexually resourceful archetype.

Value of Mixed Methods

By employing a concurrent mixed methods design, this study was able to efficiently tap into the distinctions between high and low sexually resourceful women and gain an enriched understanding of how this repertoire of skills is dynamically linked to other areas in a woman's life. The present study, through the use of a concurrent mixed methods approach, was able to harness the power of both quantitative and qualitative methods. The SCS and SRS measures distinguished the different participant cohorts, and comparative analysis of the interview data provided the level of detail that enriched our understanding of this phenomenon. Finally, by triangulating the data with the theory of self-control behavior (Rosenbaum, 1990) and script theory (Simon & Gagnon, 1986), it was possible to fully understand and model the process by which women become sexually resourceful.

Although our exploratory qualitative data collection involved a limited sample, we firmly believe that the data presented here reflect an honest and contemporary discourse among women with varying general and resourceful skills and their views and expectations about sexual behaviors. For example, we had no negative cases. All of the additional women's narratives described for the substantive model were consistent with the stories that emerged from our starting comparative analysis of the four most extreme SCS/SRS archetypes.

Limitations

The current study was conducted with a small sample of undergraduate students at a small Canadian university and therefore the experiences of the participants may not be reflective of those of the general population. Additionally, until further research can determine its broader applicability, the proposed model may be specific to only young heterosexual women and only in a North American context. The effect of sexual orientation, generation and cultural factors will need to be further explored. Having said this, the two older women, who were interviewed but excluded from our analysis, were highly generally resourceful but only moderately sexually resourceful. Although consultation with peers about sex was now less important for them, their struggles with becoming more sexually resourceful were expressed throughout their interviews. At the time of her interview, one woman was a crisis counselor and described how the training for this role helped to empower her with her current sexual relationships. Further longitudinal studies are needed to determine how sexual resourcefulness unfolds for women as they age, and to what extent having a relatively larger general repertoire of skills is important for them. Given the large number of highly and moderately generally resourceful having low levels of sexual resourcefulness skills, it is possible that for many of them that the development of their sexual resourcefulness skills are in a transitional phase. Over time, as acknowledged by our two older cases, reflection, experience and education may make them more perceptive about sexual relationships.

REFERENCES

Arnett, J. J. (1995). Adolescents' uses of media for self-socialization. *Journal of Youth and Adolescence, 24,* 519-533.

Brown, J. D. , White, A. B. , & Nikopoulou, L. (1993). Disinterest, intrigue, resistance: Early adolescent girls' use of sexual media content. In B. S. Greenberg, J. D. Brown, & N. Buerkel-Rothfuss (Eds.), *Media, sex and the adolescent* (pp. 177-195). Cresskill. NJ: Hampton Press.

Bryman, A. (2006). Integrating quantitative and qualitative research: How is it done? *Qualitative Research, 6,* 97-113.

Byers, E. S. , Sears, H. A. , & Weaver, A. D. (2008). Parents' reports of sexual communication with children in kindergarten to grade eight. *Journal of Marriage and Family, 70,* 86-96.

Connell, E. (2005). Desire as interruption: Young women and sexuality education in Ontario, Canada. *Sex Education, 5,* 253-268.

Creswell, J. W. (2003). *Research Design: Qualitative, quantitative, and mixed methods approaches (2nd ed.).* Thousand Oaks, CA: Sage.

Deardorff, J. , Gonzales, N. A. , Christopher, F. S. , Roosa, M. W. , Millsap, R. E. (2005). Early puberty and adolescent pregnancy: The influence of alcohol use. *Pediatrics, 116,* 1451-1456.

Fingerson, L. (2005). Do mothers' opinions matter in teens' sexual activity? *Journal of Family Issues, 26,* 947-974.

Gagnon, J. H. (1990). The explicit and implicit use of the scripting perspective in sex research. *Annual Review of Sex Research, 1,* 1-43.

Greene, J. C. , Benjamin, L. , & Goodyear, L. (2001). The merits of mixing methods in evaluation. *Evaluation, 7,* 25-44.

Henry, D. B. , Schoeny, M. E. , Deptula, D. P. , & Slavick, J. T. (2007). Peer selection and socialization effects on adolescent intercourse without a condom and attitudes about the costs of sex. *Child Development, 78,* 825-838.

Hittner, J. B. , & Kennington, L. E. (2008). Normative perceptions, substance use, age of substance use initiation, and gender as predictors of HIV-risky sexual behavior in a college student sample. *Journal of Applied Biobehaviorial Research, 13,* 86-101.

Humphreys, T. P. , & Kennett, D. J. (2010). The reliability and validity of instruments supporting the sexual self-control model. *The Canadian Journal of Human Sexuality, 19,* 1-13.

Humphreys, T. P. , & Kennett, D. J. (2011). The female sexual resourcefulness scale. In T. D. Fisher, C. L. Davis, W. L. Yarber, and S. L. Davis (Eds.), *Handbook of Sexuality-Related Measures* (pp. 173-176). New York: Routledge.

Hutchinson, M. K. , & Cederbaum, J. A. (2011). Talking to daddy's little girl about sex: Daughter's reports of sexual communication and support from fathers. *Journal of Family Issues, 32,* 550-572.

Kennett, D. J. , & Ackerman, M. (1995). Importance of learned resourcefulness to weight loss and early success during maintenance: Preliminary evidence. *Patient Education and Counseling, 25,* 197-203.

Kennett, D. J. , Humphreys, T. P. , & Patchell, M. (2009). The role of learned resourcefulness in helping female undergraduates deal with unwanted sexual activity. *Sex Education, 9,* 341-353.

Kennett, D. J. , O'Hagan, F. T. , & Cezer, D. (2008). Learned resourcefulness and the long-term benefits of a chronic pain management program. *Journal of Mixed Methods Research, 2,* 317-339.

Kennett, D. J. , Morris, E. , & Bangs, A. M. (2006). Learned resourcefulness and smoking cessation revisited. *Patient Education and Counseling, 60,* 206-211.

Kennett, D. J. , & Nisbet, C. (1998). The influence of body mass index and learned resourcefulness skills on body image and lifestyle practices. *Patient Education and Counseling, 33,* 1-12.

Knauss, C. , Paxton, S. J. , & Alsaker, F. D. (2008). Body dissatisfaction in adolescent boys and girls: Objectified body consciousness, internalization of the media body ideal and perceived pressure from media. *Sex Roles, 59,* 633-643.

Laumann, E. O. , & Gagnon, J. H. (1995). A sociological perspective on sexual action. In R. G. Parker, & J. H. Gagnon (Eds.), Conceiving sexuality: Approaches to sex research in a postmodern world (pp. 183-213). Florence, KY, US: Taylor & Francis.

L'Engle, K. L. , Brown, J. D. , & Kenneavy, K. (2006). The mass media are an important context for adolescents' sexual behaviour. *Journal of Adolescent Health, 38,* 186-192.

Miller, B. C. , Norton, M. C. , Curtis, T. , Hill, E. J. , Schvaneveldt, P. , & Young, M. H. (1997). The timing of sexual intercourse among adolescents: Family, peer, and other antecedents. *Youth and Society, 29,* 54-83.

Peter, J. , & Valkenburg, P. (2010). Processes underlying the effects of adolescents' use of sexually explicit internet material: The role of perceived realism. *Communication Research, 37,* 375-399.

Potard, C. , Courtois, R. , & Rusch, E. (2008). The influence of peers on risky sexual behaviour during adolescence. *The European Journal of Contraception and Reproductive Health Care, 13,* 264-270.

Preechawong, S. , Zauszniewski, J. A. , Heinzer, M. M. V. , Musil, C. M. , Keresmar, C. , & Aswinanonh, R. (2007). Relationships of family functioning, self-esteem, and resourceful coping of Thai adolescents with asthma. *Issues in Mental Health Nursing, 28,* 21-36.

Rosenbaum, M. (1980). A schedule for assessing self-control behaviours: Preliminary findings. *Behaviour Therapy, 11,* 109-121.

Rosenbaum, M. (1990). The role of learned resourcefulness in the self-control of health behaviour. In M. Rosenbaum (Ed.), *Learned resourcefulness: On coping skills, self-control and adaptive behaviour* (pp. 4-25). New York: Springer Publishing Company.

Rosenbaum, M. (2000). The self-regulation of experience: openess and construction. In P. Dewe, A. M. Leiter, & T. Cox (Eds.), *Coping and health in organizations* (pp. 51-67). London: Taylor and Francis.

Shtarkshall, R. A. , Carmel, S. , Jaffe-Hirschfield, D. , & Woloski-Wruble, A. (2009). Sexual milestones and factors associated with coitus initiation among Israeli high school students. *Archives of Sexual Behavior, 38,* 591-604.

SIECCAN (2009). Sexual health education in the schools: questions & answers (3rd edition). *The Canadian Journal of Human Sexuality, 18,* 47-60.

Simon, W. , & Gagnon, J. H. (1986). Sexual scripts: Permanence and change. *Archives of Sexual Behavior, 15,* 97-120.

Simon, W. , & Gagnon, J. H. (2003). Sexual scripts : Origins, influences, and changes. *Qualitative Sociology, 26,* 491-497.

Smylie, L. , Maticka-Tyndale, E. , & Boyd, D. (2008). Evaluation of a school-based sex education programme delivered to grade nine students in Canada. *Sex Education, 8,* 25-46.

Striegel-Moore, R. H. , McMahon, R. P. , Biro, F. M. , Schreiber, G. , Crawford, P. B. , & Voorhees, C. (2001). Exploring the relationship between timing of menarche and eating disorder symptoms in black and white adolescent girls. *International Journal of Eating Disorders, 30,* 421-433.

Tolman, D. L. , & McClelland, S. I. (2011). Normative sexuality development in adolescence: A decade of review, 2000-2009. *Journal of Research on Adolescence, 21,* 242-255.

Türkel, Y. D. , & Tezer, E. (2008). Parenting styles and learned resourcefulness of Turkish adolescents. *Adolescence, 43,* 143-152.

Ward, L. M. , & Rivadeneyra, R. (1999). Contributions of entertainment television to adolescents' sexual attitudes and expectations: The role of viewing amount versus viewer involvement. *Journal of Sex Research, 36,* 237-249.

White, R. , Tata, P. & Burns, T. (1996). Mood, learned resourcefulness and perceptions of control in type 1 diabetes mellitus. *Journal of Psychosomatic Research, 40,* 205-212.

Zauszniewski, J. A. , & Chung, C. W. (2001). Resourcefulness and health practices of diabetic women. *Research in Nursing & Health, 21,* 113-121.

Zauszniewski, J. A. , Chung, C. W. , Chang, H. J. , & Krafcik, K. (2002). Predictors of resourcefulness in school-aged children. *Issues in Mental Health Nursing, 23,* 385-401.

In: Psychology of Self-Control
Editors: A. Durante, et. al.

Chapter 2

SELF-CONTROL: AN ORPHAN CONSTRUCT IN SEARCH OF A THEORY?

Luciano L'Abate

Georgia State University
Atlanta, Georgia, U. S.

Abstract

The purpose of this chapter is to link the construct of self-control or self-regulation to a model by the same title in Relational Competence Theory (RCT; Cusinato & L'Abate, in press; L'Abate, Cusinato, Maino, Colesso, & Scilletta, 2010). Self-control, like many other ubiquitous orphan psychological constructs, such as locus of control, reactivity, resilience, and self-esteem among others, historically has not been heretofore connected usually to any specific theory in any particularly testable fashion. If and when this construct has been linked to a theory, e. g. , psychoanalysis, social learning, operant conditioning, or attachment, for instance, it has not been stated in ways that lead to empirical or experiential verification and validation, except perhaps for behavioral formulations. However, only its normative rather than non-normative aspects have been usually considered. The latter will be included here because they are an intrinsic aspect of models in RCT, especially self-report.

HISTORICAL AND SYSTEMATIC BACKGROUND

Here I shall trace chronologically the step-by-step historical and systematic background of influential and outstanding pioneers, researchers, and theorists who studied self-control from various viewpoints. According to an early view from the beginning of last century, for instance, Paulsen and Thilly (1900) argued that the chief purpose of all moral culture is to fashion the rational will so that it may become the regulative principle of the entire sphere of conduct. These authors called the virtue or excellence which regulates our behavior and conduct by the rational will, independently of momentary feelings, self-control. We may also define it as the capacity to govern life by purposes and ideals. It is the fundamental condition of all moral virtues, the fundamental precondition of all human worth, nay, the fundamental characteristic of human nature.

According to Paulsen and Thilly, self-control assumes different phases, corresponding to the different forms of impulsive life. As its two fundamental aspects we may, with the Greek moralists, designate temperance and courage. Temperance may be defined as the moral power to resist desires attracted by tempting enjoyment, when the gratification of such desires tends to endanger an essential good. Courage is the moral power to resist the natural fear of pain and danger, when the preservation of an essential good demands such resistance. The fruit of self-control, which reaches its completion in the virtues of temperance and unpretendingness, courage and perseverance, patience and tranquility, is inner peace and cheerfulness of mind. This is the path which leads to self-preservation and welfare. Wisdom is needed to find and follow it.

The psychological elements in the background of voluntary reactions can be quite clearly analyzed (Bronner, 1917). In general, control of actions is dependent upon control of the mental states leading to actions. Both emotions and ideas have a very vital relationship to behavior. Almost all emotions tend to arouse action, while the chief restraining forces lie in the realm of ideas. Without entering into any discussion of vexed points concerning "the will", it may fairly be said that defective powers of control of actions may be due, on the one hand, to inability to repress the feelings, that is, to lack of emotional control; and, on the other, to failure to arouse inhibiting ideas. From this it may be seen that defective power of control involves both emotional and ideational or volitional aspects of mental life.

According to Bronner (1917), the practical issues with which we are here concerned are recognition of the existence of this type of defect and of the need that arises for adjustment of social conditions to meet the responses that such defect calls forth. The power to awaken inhibiting ideas and to keep such thoughts in the foreground of consciousness so that they may become effective, is a power as truly characteristic of mental life as is the capacity for recalling past experience or for performing any other mental function. Then, too, there are, no doubt, inborn differences in the intensity of the emotions as well as in the capacity for resisting emotions, impulses, and desires. Situations that apparently appear the same are in reality quite unlike for different people. Similar or even identical situations arouse feelings so varied and of such different degrees of intensity that the reactions arising from them require by necessity widely varying degrees of control. Davenport (undated) has called individuals showing such defect in powers of control "the feebly inhibited".

What the inhibitory mechanism, the neural basis of inhibition, may be is discussed in all textbooks dealing with physiological psychology. The general opinion is that nervous impulses are converted into inhibition as truly as into other types of action, for action is restraint as well as movement. Whether or not it is some flaw in the neural mechanism that accounts for defects in mental control and whatever theories of inheritance of inhibition may prove true, the fact remains that the problems which arise in the case of individuals defective in control are extremely practical. Those who have dealt extensively with delinquents are familiar with the characteristics of this type of individual, their inability to resist temptations, their extreme bad temper, angry threats, and violent reactions. Examples illustrating this kind of defect are visible in Axis II, Cluster B personality disorders (Diagnostic and Statistical Manual, Mental Disorders, second edition: DSM-II).

In a series of pioneering articles, Hartshorne, May, and Maller (1929a) examined the general environment as a factor in self-control. Topics discussed included the following: (1) community differences, (2) occupational differences, (3) economic and cultural differences, (4) national differences, and (5) religious differences. Hartshorne, May, and Maller (1929b) also argued that in that decade it became apparent that self-control is not only highly specific but is also the result of miscellaneous causes, no one of which seems to stand out as a prepotent factor over others.

The strongest associations so far noted by these authors about self-control have been those of age, intelligence, sex, school experience, and such aspects of environment as are indicated by community, nationality, and the home. These associations have been bound up less closely associated with our inhibition scores than with persistence. It remains now to bring together such facts as are available regarding the relation between self-control and Sunday-school attendance, experience in clubs and summer camps, and attendance at motion picture shows. These factors also related (1929c) together with gender, physical, and emotional conditions to self-control. Topics discussed included the following: (1) sex and persistence, (2) sex and inhibition, (3) possible explanation of sex differences in self-control, (4) the physical condition, (5) the health examination, and (6) the emotional condition.

In a chapter about control of behavior, Herrick (1929a) discussed inorganic and organic control, mechanical controllers, reflex control, human control of events, mental control, and purposive self-control. In another chapter about voluntary control, Herrick (1929b) discussed will power, self control, and choice. Will power is an expression of self-control. The cultivation of will power is a creative process. We can generate this priceless power only when we have the proper machinery for it. The power of self-control is the badge of our humanity. It is the most glorious thing we have.

Developmentally, infants are creatures of impulse, but most adults are not. Older people who have difficulty controlling themselves are called "childish", and a person who is carried away and acts impulsively later condemns his own behavior as "infantile". The mentally deficient or psychotic also have difficulty in disciplining themselves, and they are usually approached condescendingly as overgrown children. Something happens to most people between infancy and adulthood. Living up to one's responsibilities is a very complex form of behavior. How does this remarkable ability develop? A definitive answer cannot be given, but there are a number of hypotheses worthy of serious consideration. Shibutani's (1961) chapter looked at the dialectic of personal growth, adjustments to significant others, participation in concerted action, and transformations of personal identity.

Stuart (1972) explained and discussed improvements in the DSM-II with a detailed outline given to its organization, and a table was included with the latest nomenclature in diagnoses with referential code numbers. This is the first reference I know of that relates self-control to psychopathology and psychiatric classification. Schulz (1976) examined some observational and correlational evidence showing the importance of hope in maintaining life and the role of hopelessness in fostering deterioration. Results of an experiment which used institutionalized older persons to test the hypothesis that hope and hopelessness were mediated by individual's cognitions about the predictability and controllability of their environments were reported. This is also the first study that related self-control to predictability and controllability, aspects of self-control that were studied in greater depth by the next contributor.

The Work of Ellen J. Langer (1983)

This researcher argued very successfully that there is no such as thing as control in and of itself, instead, there might be a delusion or illusion of "perceived control":

> "I now conceive of control as an ongoing process. People experience control as they master their internal (mental) or external environments – as they make the unfamiliar familiar "(Langer, 1983, p. 19)... The implicit definition of control employed throughout these chapters is the *active belief that one has a choice* among responses that are differentially effective in achieving the desired outcome (p. 20).

She proceeded to study experimentally "perceived control", "induced dependence", crowding and cognitive control, burglary prevention, post-divorce adaptation, reduction of psychological stress in surgical patients, the decline of control and the fall of self-esteem in aging including experimental interventions to increase personal responsibility in senior participants, studying the long term effects of control-relevant and memory improvement strategy in late adulthood and induced disability in nursing home patients. The bottom line of Langer's pioneering work has lead us to understand stress as the loss of perceived control, as in many situations, old age, and physical and psychological handicaps.

The Sociological Contribution of Jack P. Gibbs (1989)

Ignoring completely Langer's original contribution, Gibbs insisted that control was sociology's "central notion. " He reviewed basic types of control including power and attempted control as overt behavior to increase or decrease the probability of a desirable outcome (p. 23). The three key terms Gibbs considers important to define control are: deliberation, conscious anticipation, and specific consequences. Furthermore, he differentiated successful from unsuccessful, as well as intentional from unintentional control. Successful control is effective when there is repetition of the same intention when the goal of attempted control is achieved, realized, maintained, or, on the other hand, avoided when avoidance of a certain outcome is obtained.

Gibbs went on to illustrate "conspicuous features of control" in "humanoids", inanimate objects, human activities with survival or enjoyment through animals and vegetables, and humans. Of special interest to sociologists but lately of interest to psychologists (L'Abate, 2011-b), Gibbs discussed control within sociological paradigms, such as functionalism, psychoanalysis, materialism, class struggles, elitology (study of populations thought to have special endowments or characteristics), behavioral sociology, and sociobiology. He ended his contribution with chapters on future work on the efficacy of control, and the relationship between control and freedom.

It should be noted that Gibbs considered control at group and institutional levels, even though he referred to "self-control" in four instances (pp. 49, 72, 217, 218). Consequently, his contribution should be considered at the level he intended to discuss it: sociological. Nonetheless, historically, his significant work cannot be ignored for its scholarship and its implications for our understanding of control in general and self-control in particular.

The Logic of Social Control by Allan V. Horowitz (1990)

This contribution was written by another sociologist from the viewpoint of control as a legal process that includes the importance of theory:

> "The purpose of a theory is to order, predict, and explain variation. Ordering occurs through concepts that organize and categorize phenomena that are considered important for the purpose of the theory. The first task in the study of social control is to define the appropriate field of study. A concept of social control must be broad enough to embrace the wide variety of styles and forms that respond to norm violations yet precise enough to create a manageable field of study (Horowitz, 1990, p. 8). "

Horowitz proceeded to include four, extremely influential styles of social control: (1) *penal* as in courts and prison, as punishment; (2) *compensatory* as in paying back for services rendered; (3) *conciliatory* as in trying to palliate and negotiate conflicts, and (4) *therapeutic*, as in psychotherapy or psychological interventions. In addition to these four styles, Horowitz covered four different but often overlapping forms of social control, such as inaction or apathy, unilateral and bilateral social control as an exchange between parties involved, and finally trilateral forms of control emanating from different source, legal, penal, and enforcing. These styles and forms of social control require an evaluation of their effectiveness in preventing, detecting, and treating social deviance, including victim-offender relationships.

As a sociologist Horowitz was not interested in self-control *per se*. While Gibbs (1990) had four references to the self, Horowitz had none. Why then include both sociologists in a chapter dedicated to psychological self-control? That question can be answered as follows: (1) self-control cannot be considered outside the culture in which it occurs and learned, a factor that some psychologists interested in self-control usually might not include; (2) we can learn a great deal about social control that is relevant to self-control. For instance, all the notions proffered by Gibbs and Horowitz are extremely helpful (at least to me) in understanding the context of self-control as represented by our culture. This context includes also ways and means by which cultural settings attempt to achieve control in ways that can be mimicked at the personal level. For instance, when self-control is required in some churches, in other churches complete loss of control is not only acceptable but also encouraged and valued.

Desire for Control (Burger, 1992)

Finally we have a psychologist who considers personality and individual differences in actually measuring desire for control by developing and validating a scale to assess this construct. This, like Langer's acknowledged contribution about the illusion of control, is definitely an important addition to the study of self-control. Since self-control cannot be measured directly, one could argue, as Burger does, that only desire for self-control can be assessed. He quoted other researchers who distinguished between two types of control: *primary* in direct efforts to change one's environment and *secondary*, bringing ourselves into line with environmental forces (Burger, 1992).

> "The concept of personal control can be found throughout research in personality, social psychology, and clinical psychology. Although much early research suggested that the more control one has over any given event the better, more recent work has identified many exceptions (p. 8) to this rule. Nonetheless, all things being equal, people probably prefer exercising control over not exercising control...desire for control can be thought of as a very general trait relevant to a wide range of behaviors. In any given situation, the extent to which a person wants to control what happens would seem to be a crucial piece of information per predicting his or her behavior. If we can identify a person's general level of desire for control, then we should better understand what he or she does in many parts of his or her life" (p. 9).

Burger went on to validate his Desire for Control (DC) Scale in social interactions, social influence, achievement behavior and intrinsic motivation, attributions and infor-mation processing, well-being, adjustment, and health, depression, and gambling. Among many significant findings, one interesting piece of research deals with the interaction between desire for control (DC) and locus of control (LOC), producing a model (p. 146) where Internal LOC interacts with High DC to produce achievement, Internal LOC with Low DC may tend to produce anxiety, External LOC with High DC may tend to produce depression, while LOC with Low DC may produce "content" not otherwise specified.

Given the thorough research and significant results obtained by Burger, one cannot help wonder why his DC Scale has not be used more widely by psychologists. Wondering why Burger's monumental research had not been used by psychologists, I consulted four acknowledged, representative textbooks in personality theory. In one (Pervin, 1990), "control theory" was mentioned twice but desire for control was not mentioned. In a second edition of the preceding text (Pervin & John, 1999) control theory was reviewed within the effects of culture in two pages, but desire for control was not mentioned. In a third edition of the same textbook (John, Robins, & Pervin, 2008), one chapter (Ryan & Deci, 2008) considered "controlled motivation" as a component of "basic psychological needs" but with no mention of desire for control. In a fourth textbook (Hogan, Johnson, & Briggs, 1997), control was mentioned seven times, control elements once, control models once, control processes were viewed in two pages, while "controls" received one entire chapter (Mugargee, 1997). In case one wonders about whether "self-control" was even considered, Hogan et al. (1997) mentioned it once, while Pervin (1990), Pervin and John (1999), and John et al. (2008) did not mention it all. The reason for this seeming avoidance of this term is explained below.

To make sure I did not misled myself and readers, I checked these textbooks for terms synonymous with control. I found that regulation and self-regulation were indeed partially considered in one chapter (Mischel, 1990, pp. 120-125) and mentioned in various chapters of the same textbook where that chapter was published. In the second edition of this textbook, Bandura (1999) considered "self-regulatory capability" within his social-cognitive theory of personality (pp. 175-180). Additionally, Carver and Scheier (1999) devoted a whole chapter to stress, coping, and self-regulatory processes. In the third edition of the same textbook a whole chapter was dedicated to self-regulation (Gailliot, Mead, & Baumeister, 2008), emotion regulation (Gross, 2008), and self-regulatory processes (Carver, Scheier, & Fulford, 2008). By the same token, Hogan et al. (1997) had only three references (pp. 805, 806, 903) to self-regulation.

Just to make sure I did not overlook other possibly significant contributions, I consulted the monumental review of research in attachment theory (Mikulincer & Shaver, 2007). There the construct of control is apparently made synonymous with *activation* and its extremes: hyperactivating and deactivating strategies (pp. 40-42). These strategies are considered within a section on "proximity-seeking viability" (pp. 39-40) discussed before including activation. This sequence is relevant because the same sequence is followed in greater detail by Models[4 & 5] of RCT, reviewed later on in this chapter.

The foregoing search suggests that desire for control is not (yet?) considered in personality theories. However, the whole construct of control, i. e. , regulation, is given the critical importance it deserves, as promoted by contributors reviewed above and below.

Mental Control (Wegner & Pennebaker, 1993)

This important contribution is difficult to review because it includes so many important chapters about a great many topics concerned with self-control, such as thought and memory, emotion and sensation, and motivation for action. What might be relevant to self-control is the section about emotion and sensation that includes chapters on worry, depression, emotional intelligence and the self-regulation of affect, motives for inhibiting good moods and for maintaining bad moods, gender differences in the control of depression, positive illusions and affect regulation, clinical approaches to control mood, mental control of angry aggression, controlling anger and self-induced emotion change, and physical sensations and mental control.

Please note that all these contributions are related to "mental" control as being primary to the sensation and perception of feelings and emotions, providing a relevant dimension between self-control of feelings and emotions and self-control of thinking and cognitions – is this a dimension or a dichotomy? Furthermore, mental control was viewed as preceding action, as a determinant of activities and behaviors. The emotionality-rationality dimension will be considered in greater detail below and will reappear in RCT.

How and why people fail at self-regulation (Baumeister, Heatherton, & Tice, 1994)

Here is where self-control gained one more synonymous qualification: self-regulation as "the major social pathology of the present time (p. 3) ...any effort by a human being to alter his own responses...actions, thoughts, feelings, desires, and performances, such as starting, stopping or changing a process, as well as substituting one outcome or response for another (p. 7).

Mechanisms of self-regulation failure are: conflicting standards, reduction of monitorin, inadequate strength, psychological inertia, lapse-activated causal patterns, snowball effects, acquiescence, letting it happen, and misregulation. These mechanisms are apparent in controlling impulses and appetites, alcohol consumption and abuse, eating too much, smoking, gambling, shopping, and aggression. At the end, these writers considered how self-control fails and how a theory of self-control may help in cultivating self-regulation in parenting and self-improvement. Fortunately, the first author of this contribution, did not give up and continued to expand on self-regulation in the next volume.

Self-regulation (Baumeister & Vohs, 2004)

There is no question that this is a major contribution to the study, theory, and research on self-control. One cannot really study self-control without referring to it and to its many important contributions. After devoting a first section on basic regulatory processes (action, affect, cognition, strength, willpower and delay of gratification, behavioral initiation and maintenance), a second section is devoted to cognitive, physiological, and neurological dimensions of self-regulation (automatic, promotion and prevention strategies, self-efficacy beliefs, goals, social and cognitive approaches). A third section is devoted to developmental approaches of self-regulation, such as: effortful control and socialization in childhood, attentional deficits in control, early attachment processes, childhood individual characteristics and environmental contexts, and temperament. A fourth section is devoted to interpersonal dimensions of self-regulation, such as the sociometer and requirements for functional self-regulation. A fifth section is devoted to individual differences, such as gender, and appropriate balanced attention. A final sixth section is devoted to everyday problems in self-regulation, such as failures due to addictions, alcohol, eating, shopping, sex, and crime. As one can see, this contribution covers the whole waterfront of self-control topics, barred none.

Emotion Regulation (Gross, 2007; Vingerhoets et al. , 2008)

Two new contributions add another aspect and emphasis to the study of self-control, and that is: is self-control related mainly to cognition or to emotion? Here the focus shifts to emotion without, however, denying the important of cognition. The issue is which comes first? Cognition or emotion? In other works (L'Abate, 2005, 2011-a; L'Abate et al, 2010), I have emphasized the primacy of Emotionality over Rationality, as explained briefly below in regard to the first Model[1] of RCT.

Nonetheless, after an introduction about the conceptual foundations of emotion regulation, Gross included its biological bases, including the prefrontal amygdala, neural and neuropsychological processes, as well as genetics. Another section is devoted to cognitive foundations, including executive functions, explanatory style, affect regulation, and conflict monitoring. Other sections are devoted to: (1) Developmental approaches include caregiver influences, socialization of emotion regulation in the family, awareness of regular and irregular development, effortful control and its socio-emotional consequences, and aging; (2) Personality and individual differences that include temperament, defensive and motivational factors, emotional intelligence, and how emotions facilitate or impair self-regulation; (3) Social approaches include non-conscious factors, attachment strategies in adulthood, interpersonal factors, culture, and religion; (4) clinical applications include externalization disorders in children and adolescents, treatments for anxiety and mood disorders, dialectical behavior therapy, alcohol, and stress-related treatments.

The contribution by Vingerhoets et al, (2008) is simply divided into two sections, one devoted to conceptual and neurobiological issues and another to clinical perspectives and interventions. Health, coping styles and aggression, alexithymia research and health, repressive coping style and health, crying, and emotional intelligence are included in the first section. The second section includes depression, anxiety, traumas, eating disorders, health in children, crying in psychotherapy, expressive writing, and a critique of the writing technique.

This concludes an historical review of major systematic contributions to self-control, now we can review some of the issues that confront its study

Self-control and Locus of Control (LOC)

This is another of those orphans constructs that elicited and provoked a great deal of attention at the time but that fizzled with the passing of time. It was introduced in personality psychology by Julian Rotter and was influential enough to produce hundreds if not thousands of studies (Lefcourt, 1981; Phares, 1976). According to the APA Dictionary of Psychology (p. 541), LOC is "a construct used to categorize basic motivational orientations and perceptions of how much control they have over conditions of their lives. People with an external LOC tend to behave in response to external circumstances and to perceive their life outcomes as arising from factors out of their control. People with an internal LOC tend to behave in response to internal states and intensions and to perceive their life outcomes as arising from the exercise of their own agency and abilities.

To verify my rather pessimistic conclusion about its present orphan status, I consulted the same personality treatises I consulted earlier about self-control. Chapter contributors to Hogan et al.'s (1997) textbook mentioned LOC on eight different occasions in as many different chapters (pp. 152, 362, 423, 426, 552, 813, 860, 895). In its first edition (Pervin, 1990), LOC was mentioned in three instances and received one full page in a chapter by Weiner (1990) who concluded his evaluation of LOC thusly: "...there is little theoretical legacy from this research, nor any solutions to the generality of this predisposition. But there is an empirical heritage: Perceiving control over life events appears to be an important correlate of physical and mental health (p. 474). " As a result from this conclusion (or death sentence?), LOC was not mentioned in either the second (Pervin & John, 1999) or third (John, Robins, & Pervin, 2008) editions of this textbook.

Weiner's conclusion tends to support my calling LOC an orphan construct without theoretical parentage. While self-control has been on the ascent in assuming a more and more important role in personality theory, as reviewed above, as reviewed here, at the same span of time, LOC has descended into the dust bins of history. However, I do believe that its basic differentiation between internal and external LOC is relevant once we relate this focus to Model[11] of RCT presented below.

Time Discounting

Madden and Bickel (2010) presented a completely different way to look at poor self-control as impulsivity, defined as the delay discounting of future consequences. They included a vast and impressive number of contributors who attested to the empirical validity of this construct. Instead of using a simple, reaction-time measure of how fast or how slow a participants, these investigators attributed this construct to a process of delay discounting. However, such a definition is an attribution because what they actually measure is how fast or how slow one responds to an eliciting stimulus event. Yes, indeed, as we shall see below, Cluster B personality disorders do tend to react fast to emotional stimuli. Cluster C personality disorders ma tend to respond much more slowly and may be painfully aware of possible consequences of their actions, to the point of not even recting. However, whether participants discount delaying their reactions is not a process they are aware of. They tend to react? Yes. Are they aware of the consequences of their actions? Of course not. Consequently, delay discounting is an attribution that these investigators made, even though it is supported by a great deal of empirical evidence. Why not call a response fast or slow rather than attributing a process of delay discounting that occurs outside of participants' awareness?

DEFINITIONAL ISSUES

The construct of self-control is still plagued by some issues of definition where overlapping or seemingly contrasting constructs are used as synonymous or are just opposed with each other in a dichotomy rather than a continuous dimension. For instance, should we use *Self-Control* or *Self-regulation*? Could one think of self-control as a static, structural characteristic without a continuum to define it or could self-regulation imply a characteristic involving a process of ongoing monitoring? One easy way out of this conundrum is to use both as synonymous and stop quibbling about their different characteristics.

Another definitions issue relates to how differentiate *Self-* from *Social-Control?* Where does one end and the other begin? How do we know that self-control may not be due to internalized social norms unconsciously learned? This issue is relevant to internal versus external constraints where a line cannot or is difficult to draw between personal versus cultural limitations,

Perhaps the most difficult issue is to differentiate between causes, sources, or determinants of self-control. Should these determinants be *Emotional* or *Cognitive* ? Both qualifications for control are legitimate. Both, as already shown above, can provide sufficient evidence to make a case about one source being primary over the other. Rather than stick with this simplistic dichotomy, I prefer to favor Emotionality first with Rationality (Cognition) second as a developmental progression. However, I do believe that just using one or the other is limiting what we can do to understand self-control. It takes more than Emotionality or Rationality to understand self-control, as shown below in RCT.

SELF-CONTROL AND RELATIONAL COMPETENCE THEORY

Usually failures in inadequate self-control are explained away through other theoretically orphan constructs, such as learned helplessness or low-self-esteem. An orphan construct is used to explain another orphan construct! This state of theoretical affairs may be due to the apparent failure of traditional theories, such as conditioning, psychoanalysis or attachment, to explain most failures in terms of pell-mell constructs such as "unconscious", self-esteem, or "attachment. " In other words, failures in self-control are not due to the individual's own sense of responsibility but to internal or external factors ("The devil made me do it!") outside the awareness, knowledge, or motivation to change in the individual.

Therefore, this section will review in greater detail the historical and theoretical underpinnings of self-control and then present its status as Model[5] of RCT. The major characteristic of self-control is its variability within a temporal dimension defined by speed, such as (1) extremes of discharge or disinhibition, how fast and for how long one approaches or avoids another person or an object, and (2) delay, inhibition, or restraint, how slow and for how short a time, does one approach or avoid another person or an object. Consequences in either case are not usually considered because the temporal perspective may be limited or inadequate.

This formulation allows us to see personality disorders within this temporal dimension of speed and temporal orientation and perspective. For instance, DSM Axis II Cluster B personality disorders (Author, 1994) are mainly characterized by immediate discharge or impulsivity while personality disorders in Axis II Cluster C are mainly characterizes by delays, inhibitions, and procrastinations. Consequently, should we not use self-control singularly but use instead the term "self-controls" plurally? This question is raised in the sense that there may be different types of self-control depending on the individual and its immediate and distal contexts, as discussed below.

In RCT, the ability to control self is synonymous with Model[5], included after the introduction of the ability to love as in Model[4]. The rationale for placing the ability to love before the ability to control self is strictly developmental. My collaborators and I have argued (L'Abate et al. , 2010) that the infant is born first in a world of space defined by a dimension of distance with extremes in approach-avoidance. The infant then enters in a world of time defined by speed of responding with discharge, immediacy, or disinhibition at one end and delay or inhibition and constraint at the other end. Speed of responding underlies a temporal perspective characterized by past, present, and future consequences, plans and perspectives.

Both Models[4 & 5], however, are based on three preceding meta-theoretical Models[1, 2, & 3] that need a brief introduction to understand fully how self-control is located and integrated into the 16 models of RCT. In this theory, self-control is no longer an orphan. It is an integral part of RCT with direct links with preceding and following models (Cusinato & L'Abate, in press; L'Abate, 2005; L'Abate et al. , 2010).

Underlying self-control one must consider how information occurs and is processed in human beings (Model[1]). That consideration goes above and beyond the simple emotional-cognitive dichotomy of previous contributions to this topic. We receive Emotional stimuli within ourselves and from others (input) which are processed Rationally (throughput) through cognitive and intellectual processes that determine in part how we express, plan, and prepare our Activities (output) for the present and for the future. These activities are followed by Awareness (feedback) of what Self has done in the immediate and distal past (Ferrari & Sternberg, 1998), allowing us to correct and improve our behavior within how we perceive our immediate and distal Context. This ERAAwC Model[1] encapsulates most of the schools of thought and of therapy from the past to the present (L'Abate, 2005).

A second Model[2] includes levels of description and of explanation. Description includes how we present ourselves publically, our social impression-formation façade versus how we behave in the privacy of our own home and in prolonged intimate relationships: family and friends. Explanation includes how we define ourselves consciously or unconsciously, that is: our identity, positively, negatively, or anywhere in between these extremes – specifically related to how we behave and control ourselves. Our identity is determined in part by our historical, inter-generational and developmental experiences, more specifically what past and present intimates have modeled and taught us and how we have learned about to control ourselves (Bogen-schneider, Small, & Tsay, 1997).

A third Model[3] includes settings composed by home/school/work as well as lasting transit settings, such as those that allow us to go from one place to another (cars, planes, or trains though roads, airports, and hotels), and temporary transitory settings (barbershops, beauty salons, churches, malls, and shopping centers) including leisure time settings (gyms, sport arenas, and movie theaters). These settings furnish the specific and usually undefined "environment" or "situation" that interact with self-control. These settings are objective, can be recorded and photographed, and measured. This objectivity is different from the subjectivity of contexts, as included in Model[1]. How we perceive a setting is different from its objective reality. We may be afraid to fly but we still have to pay for the ticket to do it.

We may exercise self-control while we are in a church but we may loose while we are in a sport venue or while driving. In line with the original question posed at the beginning of this chapter, about using the term "self-controls" plurally rather than singularly, we may exercise self-control in some settings but not in others. Who represents the perfect model of control and restrain at work may become a tyrant at home, or a rage-full driver on the road. How can we understand and predict how we control ourselves unless we consider how we process information, how we present ourselves publically and privately, and where, in which setting we control or fail to control ourselves?

For reasons of space I can only summarize models that precede Model[5] but not all the models that follow it, except for some that are more relevant to self-control than others. For instance, Model[9] differentiates among three styles in intimate relationships: (1) Conductive-Creative (CC), where self-control would be at its optimal best and highest possible level; (2) Reactive-Repetitive (RR), where self-control would be borderline and selective according to which setting seems more appropriate to the individual; and (3) Abusive-Apathetic (AA), where self-control is extreme in its intensity, either too much or too little control, with glaring contradictions and inconsistencies in its expression.

Another Model[10] about interactions based an arithmetical progression and ratios of helpful to hurtful feelings expands on those Styles by linking CC to Multiplicative/Additive interactions, where self-control is expressed and shared positively with Others, RR is linked with static positive and static negative interactions, where self-control is borderline and present in most relational conflicts, and AA is linked to subtractive and divisive interactions, where self-control might be seemingly inexistent or expressed along a dimension of complete Apathy to extreme Abuse.

A Selfhood Model[11] provides an additional way of looking a self-control according to four relational propensities based on how a sense of importance is bestowed on Self and intimate Others. When a sense of importance is bestowed positively on Self and Others, a relational propensity emerges called *Selfulness*, where self-control is appropriate and adequate. When a sense of importance is bestowed positively on Self and negatively on Others, a relational propensity called *Selfishness* emerges where self-control is selective, minimal, inconsistent, and oftentimes expressed in explosive anger against others, reaching murder in its extremes. When a sense of importance is bestowed negatively on Self and positively on Others, a propensity called *Selflessness* emerges where self-control is high and usually shown in sadness, depression, and in its extremes, suicide. When a sense of importance is bestowed negatively on both Self and Others a relational *No-self* propensity emerges that in its extremes becomes psychopathology, where self-control is extreme to the point of apathy and in some cases, as in manic episodes, absent.

Model[12] about Priorities includes other constructs such as aspirations, attitudes, goals, needs, plans, and preparations for actions. Priorities can deal with Self and intimate Others, general and specific, and about which Settings (Model[3]) are more important to the individual. If the two major goals of life are Survival and Enjoyment, for instance, self-control may be restrained in working for Survival goals and rather open when trying to enjoy life. A Model[16] about Negotiation is directly derived from Model[5]. It takes a great deal of self-control to negotiate successfully. For a more complete expositions of these models, the reader might consult more detailed explanations of RCT (Cusinato & L'Abate, in press; L'Abate et al. , 2010).

Now that the theoretical groundwork has been set, we can start at considering self-control as it applies to functional and dysfunctional populations, according to RCT.

Self-control in Functional Relationships

As discussed in selected models of RCT, self-control can be viewed redundantly from various vantage points, including Selfulness where both parties involved in a transaction win, as in prosocial behavior, solidarity (Fetchenhauser & Dunning, 2006; Lindenberg, 2006; Lindenberg, Fetchenhauser, Flache, & Buunk, 2006), and altruism (Batson, 1991; Ozinga, 1999; Post, 2007; Post, Underwood, Schloss, & Hurlbut, 2002; Sober & Wilson, 1998). I am citing all these references not only to indicate how important this relational propensity is but also to illustrate how these many references refer to normative rather than non-normative behavior, as discussed below. In other words, all these references assume that self-control is necessary for prosocial, solidarity, and altruism to occur in most normative relationships, with no attention paid to dysfunctional or even pathological expressions of self-control. Here is where internal LOC is firmly established and expressed as a strong ability to control and regulate self.

Self-control in Externalizations: Axis II, Cluster B

In Selfishness, one wins at the expense of the other, where discharge or disinhibition (Model[5]) and reactivity (Model[9]) are present: "I win, you lose". "I am more important than you are". "I am not responsible, others (partners, society, legal system) are respon-sible for my behavior". Here is where LOC is completely external. This relational propensity, where self-control is minimal and selective (certainly not in a court of law…) but blaming external targets for responsibility of one's (mis)behavior is maximal. This tendency to externalize one' behavior by blaming others, leads to acting out, aggression, hostility, and in its extremes, theft, vandalism, and murder, characterized by impulsivity (L'Abate, 1994; Mullin & Hinshaw, 2007; Nigg, Carr, Martel, & Henderson, 2007; Veenstra, 2006). This means acting without a temporal perspective with no consideration of future consequences from one's present or past actions (Strathman & Joireman, 2005). If I were to cite all the literature to support this conclusion, I would have to write a separate chapter or volume. Most of this literature relevant to this relational propensity has been cited in previous publications preceding RCT (L'Abate, 2005; L'Abate et al. , 2010), as well as in a recent review about gender differences in externalizations (L'Abate, van Eigen, & Rigamonti, 2011).

Self-control in Internalizations: Axis II, Cluster C

At the other extreme in a temporal dimension of speed, as in Selflessness visible in Cluster C personality disorders, such as anxiety and depression. These disorders are characterized by inhibitions and restraints at the cost of the individual's well-being (Bekker, & Spoor, 2008; Engle et al. ,2005; Gorfein & MacLeod, 2007; Mukargee, 1997; Redick, Heitz, & Engle, 2007), where one loses by allowing someone else to win at one's expense. When inhibitions are equated with "repressive coping" there is no doubt that an individual's health may be imperiled (Myers, Burns, Derakshan, Elfant, Eysenck, & Phipps, 2008). This relational propensity is also visible through procrastination, one important form of inhibition (Ferrari, Johnson, & McCown, 1995, pp. 137-167). LOC here is also external, not negatively as present in Cluster B disorders, but positively toward others and negatively toward self. Furthermore, evidence is mounting about constraints due to emotion-context-insensitivity in depression (Rodebaugh & Heimberg, 2008; Rottenberg & Vaughan, 2008). This evidence takes us back to Model[1] where Context is included in the five ERAAwC components.

Self-control in Severe Psychopathology: Axis II, Cluster A and Axis I

In this relational propensity of No-self, are included most severe pathological disorders, such as severe depressions, bipolar disorders, borderline personality disorders, and the schizophrenias, where extremes of self-control are clearly evident and in need of specifically tailored treatment protocols (Linehan, Bohus, & Lynch, 2007). One of its major characteristic is an inability to be aware of one's serious condition and not following medical prescriptions and treatments, that is: denying being sick: "We both lose".

Here we need to differentiate functional, that is, non-organic disorders from disorders based on clearly organic causes, such as dementia and Alzheimer (Faust & Balota, 2007). In either conditions, self-control is extreme in either direction of immediate discharge and prolonged delay, to the point of being unpredictable. One cannot safely predict when individuals in this relational propensity can lose self-control suddenly and surprisingly or how long will complete apathy and restraint last.

HOW TO IMPROVE DEFECTIVE SELF-CONTROL

As diet and exercise, stress-reduction, weight-control, and the obesity epidemic have achieved national and international prominence the importance of learning how to control oneself through relaxation and auto-regulation do not need further explication (Akhondzadeh, 2007; Finke & Huston, 2007; Giovannucci, 2007; Katz, Yeh, O'Connoll, & Faridi, 2007). The construct of self-control, therefore, has reached an intentionally crucial levels to promote physical and mental health (Anderson, 2007; Calogero & Pedrotty, 2007; Dulicai & Hill, 2007; MGrady, 2007). There is a plethora of available ways to learn to control oneself. The major issue here is motivation to change for the better (Harwood & L'Abate, 2010). For a quick but well-concise summary of mental exercises, including meditation, as well as breathing and progressive muscular relaxation, interested readers/professions may consult the *Harvard Men's Health Watch*, Volume 15, Number 7, February 2011.

Historically, however, an inevitable struggle between individuals and the several resources that go to make their individualities, begins in all of us at at our birth, and continues so long as our lives in the flesh continue (Trumbull, 1890). At the time, Trumbull did not discriminate between genders, as done in the past, using only the male noun and adjective rather then referring to both genders (n/a). On the outcome of this struggle depends the ultimate character of the one who struggles. As a matter of fact, the issue of the life-long battle is ordinarily settled in childhood. A child who is trained to self-control – as a child may be – is already a true person in fitness for humanself-mastery. A person who was not trained, in childhood, to self-control, remains hopelessly a child in continous combat with oneelf; and one can never regain the vantage-ground which childhood gave to him or her, in the battle which then opened before both genders, and in the thick of which one still finds oneself. It is in a child's earlier struggles with oneself that help can easiest be given to him or her. and that it is of greatest value for one's own developing of character.

According to Trumbull (1890), a child's first struggle with oneself ought to be in the direction of controlling one's impulse to give full play to his/her lungs and her/his muscles at the prompting of her/his nerves. As soon as a child is able to understand what is said to him/her, s/he ought to be taught and trained to control the impulse to cry and writhe under the pressure of physical pain. Coaxing and rewarding a child into quiet at such a time is not what is needed; but it is the encouraging a child into an intelligent control of oneself, that is to be aimed at by the wise parent. That control of oneself which is secured by a child in his/her intelligent repression of an impulse to cry and writhe in physical pain, is of advantage to the child in all his/her life-long struggle with oneself; and s/he should be trained in the habit of making one's self-control available to him/her/ in this struggle. A parent ought to help her/his child to refrain from laughing when s/he ought not to laugh; from crying when s/he ought not to cry; from speaking when s/he ought not to speak.

Goldfried and Merbaum (1973) highlighted important trends in background theory, current research status, and practical clinical applications of self-control over personal choice and behavior. Case studies were included which provided concrete examples of the utility of self-control procedures. In line with self-control procedures, Jonas (1973) summarized occidental and oriental experiments in biofeedback control of visceral processes. Medical applications and Zen and Yoga approaches to bodily phenomena (e. g. , blood pressure) were discussed, anticipating current interests and research on relaxation and mindfulness. In line with behavioral-operant conditioning principles, Foster (1974) presented a programmed text on principles of self-reinforcement and behavior modification. Methods of changing, measuring, and maintaining behavior changes and designing self-control programs were described.

Education was conceived as the way to teach self-control from infancy. Radin and Wittes (1974), for instance, discussed the findings, impact, and implications of the Michigan Early Education Program involving 100 4-yr-old disadvantaged children during the 1967-1968 school year. The project developed a preschool curriculum, based primarily on Piaget's theory of the sequential development of intelligence, to use in the classroom and in a home tutorial setting; and also developed a group parent education program which used behavior modification principles to teach mothers how to foster the growth of self-discipline in their children.

Fagen, Long, and Stevens (1975), in another instance, presented a 3-part, structured, integrated curriculum for the development of self-control. Part 1 presented the theoretical and conceptual structure upon which the curriculum is based; Part 2 described the 8 curriculum areas and their subsidiary units and tasks; and Part 3 described important issues pertaining to self-control curriculums in general. Novaco (1975) examined the extent to which cognitive processes and relaxation techniques could be therapeutically used to regulate the experience and expression of anger for 34 persons having anger control problems. Results indicated that cognitive control procedures can be effectively used to regulate anger arousal.

Wheeler (1976) offered a self-improvement program based on principles of behavior modification and insights from cognitive psychology. Among the topics discussed were: (1) biological monitoring and feedback, (2) fears and phobias, (3) relaxation and hypnosis, (4) modifying the intellect, and (5) self-control of success.

Up to the present, talking has heretofore assumed to be the best traditional if not the only medium of communication, education, and healing, either in expensive individual face-to-face psychotherapy, or in groups or talk-based anger-management training formats, for instance. In the last generation, however, writing in general and distance writing in particular are fast becoming the major medium of communication, education, and healing in mental health for this century. Distance writing, however, can include a variety of approa-ches, including autobiographical, diary-keeping, expressive, program-med. Many others approaches are occurring every day on the Internet, not to speak of psychotherapeutic approaches online that mimic (without pre-post intervention evaluation) traditional face-to-face, talk-based psychotherapy (L'Abate & Sweeney, 2011; Sodano, Bonadies, Di Trani, 2008).

Given this general background, how can defective self-control be improved? In two ways. In my past clinical practice, I went against the widespread Skinnerian operant conditioning practice to achieve control through rewards and reinforcements at the end of a sequence of actions.

Instead, I insisted (L'Abate, 1994) that control is learned and achieved when we start something, not when we end it. Consequently, the principle of "If you want to stop it start it!" is built in many homework assignments in interactive practice exercises described below (L'Abate, 2011c). In this Sourcebook, self-control is learned through starting and repeating undesirable behavior to the point that participants have learned to control it.

Interactive practice exercises (IPEs), called also workbooks, are based on programmed systematic questions and tasks that force participants to process and think about any imaginable topic known to us (L'Abate, 2011c). There are workbooks for lifelong learning in individuals, couples, and families without any diagnostic label. There are workbooks that cover most conditions included in the DSM manual (Author, 1994) in its most recent versions, as well as IPES derived from most well-know single- and multiple-score psychological tests and factor-analyses. Relevant to defective self-control in Cluster B and Cluster C personality disorders, there are workbooks that train participants (individual children, youth, adults, couples, and families) to learn to control impulsivity, anti-social tendencies, as well as anxieties and depressions, as well as workbooks for severe psychopathology.

CONCLUSION

From what has been covered in this chapter, we can conclude that self-control is no longer an orphan. It is indeed a very important psychological construct that achieves even greater value when embedded in Relational Competence Theory. Self-control can be improved when necessary and if motivation to change for the better is present.

REFERENCES

Akhondzadeh, S. (2007). Herbal medicines in the treatment of psychiatric and neurological disorders. In L. L'Abate (Ed.), *Low-cost approaches to promote physical and mental health* (pp. 119-138). New York: Springer-Science.

Anderson, J. S. (2007). Pleasant, pleasurable, and positive activities. In L. L'Abate (Ed.), *Low-cost approaches to promote physical and mental health* (pp. 201-217). New York: Springer-Science.

Author. (1994). *Diagnostic and statistical manual of mental disorders.* Washington, DC: American Psychiatric Association.

Bandura, A. (1999). Social-cognitive theory of personality. In L. A. Pervin, & O. P. John (Eds), *Handbook of personality: Theory and research* (pp. 154-196). New York: Guilford.

Barch, D. M. , & Braver, T. S. (2005). Cognitive control and schizophrenia: Psychological and neurological mechanisms. In R. W. Engle, G. Sedek, U. von Hecker, & D. N. McIntosh (Eds.), *Cognitive limitations in aging and psychopathology* (pp. 122-159). New York: Cambridge University Press.

Batson, C. D. (1991). *The altruism question: Toward a social-psychological answer.* Hillsdale, NJ: Erlbaum.

Baumeister, R. F. , Heatherton, T. F. , & Tice, D. M. (1994). *Losing control: How and why people fail at self-regulation.* San Diego, CA: Academic Press.

Baumeister, R. F. , & Vohs, K. D. (Eds.). (2004). *Handbook of self-regulations: Research, theory, and applications.* New York: Guilford.

Bekker, M. H. J. , & Spoor, S. T. P. (2008). Emotional inhibition, health, gender, and eating disorders: The role of (over)sensitivity to others. In A. Vingerhoets, I. Nyklicek, & J. Denollet (Eds.), *Emotion regulation: Conceptual and clinical issues* (pp. 170-183). New York: Springer-Science.

Bogenschneider, K. , Small, S. A. , & Tsay, J. C. (1997). Child, parent, and contextual influences on perceived parenting competence among parents of adolescents. *Journal of Marriage and the Family, 59,* 345-362.

Bronner, A. F. (1917). Defects in mental control. In A. F. Bronner (Ed.), *The psychology of special abilities and disabilities* (pp. 166-195).

Burger, J. M. (1992). *Desire for control: Personality, social, and clinical perspectives.* New York: Plenum.

Calogero, R. , & Pedrotty, K. (2007). Daily practices for mindful exercise. In L. L'Abate (Ed.), *Low-cost approaches to promote physical and mental health* (pp. 141-159). New York: Springer-Science.

Carver, C. S. , & Scheier, M. F. (1999). Stress, coping, and self-regulatory processes. In L. A. Pervin, & O. P. John (Eds.), *Handbook of personality: Theory and research* (pp. 553-575). New York: Guilford.

Carver, C. S. , Scheier, M. F. , & Fulford, D. (2008). Self-regulatory processes, stress, and coping. In O. P. John, R. W. Robins, & L. A. Pervin (Eds.), *Handbook of personality: Theory and research* (pp. 472-491). New York: Guilford.

Cusinato, M. , & L'Abate, L. (Eds.). (in press). *Advances in relational competence theory: With special attention to alexithymia.* New York: Nova Science Publishers.

Dulicai, D. , & Hill, E. S. (2007). Expressive movement. In L. L'Abate (Ed.), *Low-cost approaches to promote physical and mental health* (pp. 177-199). New York: Springer-Science.

Engle, R. W. , Seek, G. , von Hacker, U. , & McIntosh, D. N. (Eds.). (2005). *Cognitive limitations in aging and psychopathology.* New York: Cambridge University Press.

Fagen, S. A. , Long, N. J. , & Stevens, D. J. (1975). *Teaching children self-control: Preventing emotional and learning problems in the elementary school.* Oxford England: Charles E. Merrill.

Faust, M. E. , & Balota, D. A. (2007). Inhibition, facilitation, and attentional control in dementia of the Alzheimer's type: The role of unifying principles in cognitive theory development. In D. S. Gorfein & C. M. MacLeod (Eds.), *Inhibition in cognition* (pp. 213-237). Washington, DC: American Psychological Association.

Ferrari, M. , & Sternberg, R. J. (Eds.). (1998). *Self-awareness: Its nature and development.* New York: Guilford.

Ferrari, J. R. , Johnson, J. L. , & McCown, W. G. (1995). *Procrastination and task avoidance: Theory, research, and treatment.* New York: Plenum.

Fetchenhauser, D. , & Dunning, D. (2006). Perceptions of prosociability and solidarity in self and others. In D. Fetchenhauser, A. Flache, A. P. Buunk, & S. Lindenberg (Eds.), *Solidarity and prosocial behavior: An integration of sociological and psychological perspectives* (pp. 61-74). NewYork: Springer-Science.

Finke, M. S. , & Huston, S. J. (2007). Low-cost obesity interventions: The market for foods. In L. L'Abate (Ed.), *Low-cost approaches to promote physical and mental health* (pp. 73-85). New York: Springer-Science.

Foster, C. (1974). *Developing self-control.* Oxford England: Behaviordelia.

Gailliot, M. T. , Mead, N. L. , & Baumeister, R. F. (2008). Self-regulation. In O. P. John, R. W. Robins, & L. A. Pervin (Eds.), *Handbook of personality: Theory and research* (pp. 472-491). New York: Guilford.

Gibbs, J. P. (1989). *Control: Sociology's central notion.* Urbana, IL: University of Illinois Press.

Giovannucci, E. (2007). Vitamins, minerals, and health. In L. L'Abate (Ed.), *Low-cost approaches to promote physical and mental health* (pp. 103-117). New York: Springer-Science.

Goldfried, M. R. , & Merbaum, M. (1973). *Behavior change through self-control.* Oxford England: Holt, Rinehart & Winston.

Gorfein, D. S. , & MacLeod, C. M. (Eds.). (2007). *Inhibition in cognition.* Washington, DC: American Psychological Association.

Gross, J. J. (Ed.). (2007). *Handbook of emotion regulation.* New York: Guilford.

Gross, J. J. (2008). Emotion and emotion regulation. In O. P. John, R. W. Robins, & L. Pervin (Eds.), *Handbook of personality: Theory and research* (pp. 701-724). New York: Guilford.

Hartshorne, H. , May, M. A. , & Maller, J. B. (1929a). General environment as a factor in self-control. In H. Hartshorne, M. A. May, J. B. Maller (Eds.), *Studies in the nature of character, II Studies in service and self-control* (pp. 390-406). New York,: MacMillan.

Hartshorne, H. , May, M. A. , & Maller, J. B. (1929b). Out-of-school experience as a factor in self-control. In H. Hartshorne, M. A. May, J. B. Maller (Eds.), *Studies in the nature of character, II Studies in service and self-control* (pp. 418-427). New York: MacMillan.

Hartshorne, H. , May, M. A. , & Maller, J. B. (1929c). Sex and physical and emotional condition in relation to self-control. In H. Hartshorne, M. A. May, J. B. Maller (Eds.), *Studies in the nature of character, II Studies in service and self-control* (pp. 380-389). New York: MacMillan.

Harwood, T. M. , & L'Abate, L. (2010). *Self-help in mental health: A critical evaluation*. New York: Springer-Science.

Herrick, C. (1929a). Control of behavior. In C. Herrick (Ed.), *The thinking machine* (pp. 307-319). Chicago, IL: University of Chicago Press.

Herrick, C. (1929b). Voluntary control. In C. Herrick (Ed.), *The thinking machine* (pp. 320-333). Chicago, IL: University of Chicago Press.

Hogan, R. , Johnson, J. , & Briggs, S. (Eds). (1997). *Handbook of personality psychology*. San Diego, CA: Academic Press.

Horwitz, A. V. (1990). *The logic of social control*. New York: Plenum.

John, O. P. , Robins, R. W. , & Pervin, L. A. (Eds.). (2008). *Handbook of personality: Theory and research*. New York: Guilford.

Jonas, G. (1973). *Visceral learning: Toward a science of self-control*. Oxford England: Viking.

Joormann, J. (2005). Inhibition, rumination, and mood regulation in depression. In R. W. Engle, G. Sedek, U. von Hecker, & D. N. McIntosh (Eds.), *Cognitive limitations in aging and psychopathology* (pp. 275-312). New York: Cambridge University Press.

Katz, D. L. , Yeh, M-C. , O'Connell, M. , & Faridi, Z. (2007). Diets, health, and weight control: What do we know? In L. L'Abate (Ed.), *Low-cost approaches to promote physical and mental health* (pp. 47-71). New York: Springer-Science.

L'Abate, L. (1984). Beyond paradox: Issues of control. *American Journal of Family Therapy, 12*, 12-20.

L'Abate, L. (1994). A family theory of impulsivity. In W. McCown, J. L. Johnson, & M. B. Shure (Eds.). *The impulsive client: Theory, research and treatment* (pp. 93-117). Washington, D. C. : American Psychological Association.

L'Abate, L. (2005). *Personality in intimate relationships: Socialization and psycho-pathology*. New York: Springer-Science.

L'Abate, L. (2011a). *Hurt feelings: Theory and research in intimate relationships*. New York: Cambridge University Press.

L'Abate, L. (2012b). *Paradigms in theory construction*. New York: Springer-Science.

L'Abate, L. (2011c). *Sourcebook of interactive practice exercises in mental health.* NewYork: Springer-Science.

L'Abate, L. , Cusinato, M. , Maino, E. , Colesso, W. , & Scilletta, C. (2010). *Relational competence theory: Research and mental health applications.* New York: Springer-Science.

L'Abate, L. , & Sweeney, L. G. (Eds.). (2011). *Research on writing approaches in mental health.* Bingley, UK: Emerald Group Publishing Limited.

L'Abate, L. , van Eigen, A. , & Rigamonti, S. (2011). Relational and cross-cultural perspectives on non-violent externalizing personality disordered women: Introduction to research. *American Journal of Family Therapy, 39,* 325-347.

Langer, E. J. (1983). *The psychology of control.* Beverly Hills, CA: Sage.

Lefcourt, H. M. (Ed.). (1981). *Research with the locus of control construct.* New York: Academic Press.

Lindenberg, S. (2006). Prosocial behavior, solidarity, and framing processes. In D. Fetchenhauser, A. Flache, A. P. Vuunk. & S. Lindenberg (Eds.), *Solidarity and prosocial behavior: An integration of sociological and psychological perspectives* (pp. 23-44). NewYork: Springer-Science.

Linehan, M. M. , Bohus, M. , & Lynch, T. R. (2007). Dialectical behavior therapy for pervasive emotion dysregulation. In J. J. Gross (Ed.), *Handbook of emotion regulation* (pp. 523-540). New York: Guilford.

Lindenberg, S. , Fetchenhauser, D. , Flache, A. , & Buunk, B. (2006). Solidarity and prosocial behavior: A framing approach. In D. Fetchenhauser, A. Flache, A. P. Vuunk. & S. Lindenberg (Eds.), *Solidarity and prosocial behavior: An integration of sociological and psychological perspectives* (pp. 3-19). NewYork: Springer-Science.

Madden, G. L. , & Bickel, W. K. (Eds). (2010). *Impulsivity: The behavioral and neuro-logical science of discounting.* Washington, DC: American Psychological Association.

McGrady, A. (2007). Relaxation and meditation. In L. L'Abate (Ed.), *Low-cost approaches to promote physical and mental health* (pp. 161-175). New York: Springer-Science.

Mikulincer, M. , & Shaver, P. R. (2007). *Attachment in adulthood: Structure, dynamics, and change.* New York: Guilford.

Mischel, W. (1990). Personality dispositions revisited and revised: A view after three decades. In L. A. Pervin (Ed.), *Handbook of personality theory and research* (pp. 111-134). New York: Guilford.

Mugargee, E. I. (1997). Internal inhibitions and controls. In R. Hogan, J. , Johnson, & S. Briggs (Eds), *Handbook of personality psychology* (581-614). San Diego, CA: Academic Press.

Mullin, B. C. , & Hinshaw, S. P. (2007). Emotion regulation and externalizing disorders in children and adolescents. In J. J. Gross (Ed.), *Handbook of emotion regulation* (pp. 523-540). New York: Guilford.

Myers, L. B. , Burns, J. W. , Derakshan, N. , Elfant, E. , Eysenck, M. W. , & Phipps, S. (2008). Current issues in repressive coping and health. In A. Vingerhoets, I. Nyklicek, & J. Denollet (Eds.), Emotion regulation: Conceptual and clinical issues (pp. 69-86). New York: Springer-Science.

Nigg, J. T. , Carr, L. , Martel, M. , & Henderson, J. M. (2007). Concepts of inhibition and developmental psychopathology. In D. S. Gorfein & C. M. MacLeod (Eds.), *Inhibition in cognition* (pp. 259-277). Washington, DC: American Psychological Association.

Novaco, R. W. (1975). *Anger control: The development and evaluation of an experimental treatment.* Oxford England: Lexington.

Oziga, J. R. (1999). *Altruism.* Westpost, CT: Praeger.

Paulsen, F. , & Thilly, F. (1900). The education of the will and the discipline of the feelings, or self-control. In F. Paulsen, F. Thilly (Eds.), *A system of ethics* (pp. 483-504). New York, NY: Charles Scribner's Sons.

Pervin, L. A. (Ed.). (1990). *Handbook of personality theory and research.* New York: Guilford.

Pervin, L. A. , & John, O. P. (Eds.). (1999). *Handbook of personality: Theory and research.* New York: Guilford.

Phares, E. J. (1976). *Locus of control in personality.* Morristown, N. J. : General Learning Press.

Post, S. G. (Ed.). (2007). *Altruism & health: Perspectives from empirical research*. New York: Oxford University Press.

Post, S. G. , Underwood, L. G. , Schloss, J. P. , & Hurlbut, W. B. (Eds.). (2002). *Altruism and altruistic love: Science, philosophy, and religion in dialogue*. New York: Oxford University Press.

Radin, N. , & Wittes, G. (1974). Integrating divergent theories in a compensatory preschool program. In P. Glasser, R. Sarri, R. Vinter (Eds.), *Individual change through small groups* New York: Free Press.

Redick, T. S. , Heitz, R. P. , & Engle, R. W. (2007). Working memory capacity and inhibition: Cognitive and social consequences. In D. S. Gorfein & C. M. MacLeod (Eds.), *Inhibition in cognition* (pp. 125-142). Washington, DC: American Psychological Association.

Rodebaugh, T. L. , & Heimberg, R. G. (2008). Emotion regulation and the anxiety disorders: Adopting a self-regulation perspective. In A. Vingerhoets, I. Nyklicek, & J. Denollet (Eds.), *Emotion regulation: Conceptual and clinical issues* (pp. 125-138). New York: Springer-Science.

Rottenberg, J. , & Vaughan, C. (2008). Emotion expression in depression: Emerging evidence for emotion-context-insensitivity. In A. Vingerhoets, I. Nyklicek, & J. Denollet (Eds.), *Emotion regulation: Conceptual and clinical issues* (pp. 140-148). New York: Springer-Science.

Ryan, R. M. , & Deci, E. L. (2008). Self-determination theory and the role of basic psychological needs in personality and the organization of behavior. In O. P. John, R. W. Robins, & L. A. Pervin (Eds.), *Handbook of personality: Theory and research* (pp. 654-678). New York: Guilford.

Schulz, R. (1976). Some life and death consequences of perceived control. In J. S. Carroll, J. W. Payne, J. S. Carroll, J. W. Payne (Eds.), *Cognition and social behavior* (pp. 135-154). Oxford England: Erlbaum.

Shibutani, T. (1961). The development of self-control. In T. Shibutani (Ed.), *Society and personality: An interactionist approach to social psychology* (pp. 502-534). Englewood Cliffs, NJ: Prentice-Hall.

Sober, E. , & Wilson, D. S. (1998). *Unto others: The evoluation and psychology of unselfish behavior.* Cambridge, MA: Harvard University Press.

Solano, L. , Bonadies, M. , & Di Trani, M. (2008). Writing for all, for some, or for no one? Some thoughts on the applications and evaluations of the writing technique. In A. Vingerhoets, I. Nyklicek, & J. Denollet (Eds.), *Emotion regulation: Conceptual and clinical issues* (pp. 125-138). New York: Springer-Science.

Stratthman, A. , & Joireman, J. (Eds.). (2005). *Understanding behavior in the context of time.* Mahwah, NJ: Erlbaum.

Stuart, R. B. (1972). Situational versus self-control. In R. D. Rubin, H. Fensterheim, J. D. Henderson, L. P. Ullmann (Eds.), *Advances in behavior therapy: Proceedings of the Fourth Conference of the Association for Advancement of Behavior Therapy* Oxford England: Academic Press.

Trumbull, H. (1890). Training a child to self-control. In H. Trumbull (Ed.), *Hints on child-training* (pp. 93-100). New York, NY: Charles Scribner's Sons.

Van der Zee, K. , & Perugini, M. (2006). Personality and solidarity behavior. In D. Fetchenhauser, A. Flache, A. P. Buunk, & S. Lindenberg (Eds.), *Solidarity and prosocial behavior: An integration of sociological and psychological perspectives* (pp. 77-92). NewYork: Springer-Science.

Veenstra, R. (2006). The development of Dr. Jekyll and Mr. Hyde: Prosocial and anti-social behavior in adolescence. In D. Fetchenhauser, A. Flache, A. P. Buunk, & S. Lindenberg (Eds.), *Solidarity and prosocial behavior: An integration of sociological and psychological perspectives* (pp. 93-108). NewYork: Springer-Science.

Verhaeghen, P. , Cerella, J. , Bopp, K. L. , & Basak, C. (2005). Aging and varieties of cognitive control: A review of meta-analyses on resistance to interference, coordination, and task switching, and an experimental exploration of age-sensitivity in the newly identified process of focus switching. In R. W. Engle, G. Sedek, U. von Hecker, & D. N. McIntosh (Eds.), *Cognitive limitations in aging and psychopathology* (pp. 160-189). New York: Cambridge University Press.

Vingerhoets, A. , Nyklicek, I. , & Denollet, J. (Eds.). (2008). *Emotion regulation: Conceptual and clinical issues*. New York: Springer-Science.

Wegner, D. M. , & Pennebaker, J. W. (Eds.). (1993). *Handbook of mental control*. Englewood Cliffs, NJ: Prentice Hall.

Weiner, B. (1990). Attribution in personality psychology. In L. A. Pervin (Ed.), *Handbook of personality theory and research* (pp. 465-485). New York: Guilford.

West, R. , & Bowry, R. (2005). The aging of cognitive control: Studies in conflict processing, goal neglect, and error monitoring. In R. W. Engle, G. Sedek, U. von Hecker, & D. N. McIntosh (Eds.), *Cognitive limitations in aging and psychopathology* (pp. 97-121). New York: Cambridge University Press.

Wheeler, D. R. (1976). *Control yourself*. Oxford England: Nelson-Hall.

In: Psychology of Self-Control
Editors: A. Durante, et. al.

ISBN: 978-1-61470-881-0
© 2012 Nova Science Publishers, Inc.

Chapter 3

SOCIOTROPY-AUTONOMY AND SELF-CONTROL

Toru Sato, Brittany A. Harman, Casey Alan Murray and Colleen M. Grookett

Department of Psychology
Shippensburg University
1871 Old Main Drive, Shippensburg, U. S.

Abstract

Research by Baumeister et al. (1998) suggests the existence of a limited source of mental energy that can be used for self-control. Personality differences, however, can influence how rapidly this mental energy is lost after engaging in tasks requiring self-control (Tangney, Baumeister, & Boone, 2004). Additionally, recent research suggests that personality differences in sociotropy and autonomy can contribute to how an individual attempts to replenish the lost mental energy (Sato, Harman, Donohoe, Weaver, & Hall, 2010). In his theory of depression, Beck (1983) suggests that individuals high in the personality dimensions of sociotropy and autonomy are at an increased risk of depression. Highly sociotropic individuals have a strong need for social acceptance and are more likely to resort to seeking help from others in stressful situations (Beck, 1983). Conversely, highly autonomous individuals tend to place great emphasis on personal accomplishments and may feel de-energized and depressed when they believe they have failed (Beck, 1987). This chapter summarizes two studies which investigate how highly sociotropic and autonomous individuals differ in their response to the loss of mental energy following tasks that require active self-control. Study 1 investigated whether individuals high in sociotropy or autonomy have less mental energy to begin with and whether they expend more mental energy when they engage in tasks that require self-control than those low in the respective personality traits. Study 2 examined how the loss of mental energy affects the motivation of individuals high in sociotropy and autonomy compared to those low in the respective personality dimensions. The results of Study 1 suggest that while highly sociotropic individuals have less mental energy to begin with than those low in sociotropy, they may not expend more mental energy while engaging in tasks requiring self-control. Study 2 revealed two interesting results. The first was that highly autonomous individuals have more motivation to perform well on personal tasks requiring self-control than individuals low in autonomy overall. The second interesting result was that highly autonomous individuals' motivation to perform well on personal tasks increases more than those low in autonomy following a task requiring high levels of self-control.

Keywords: Personality, Sociotropy, Autonomy, Self-Control, Ego depletion, Motivation.

Individuals exert self-control on a daily basis in a multitude of ways. They reject behaviors that might feel immediately pleasant or gratifying but which have negative long-term consequences, such as sleeping late instead of getting to work on time, eating healthy foods instead of more appealing foods that are high in calories, or controlling their emotional or verbal responses in situations when they may prefer to react with frustration or anger. These types of self-regulatory behaviors that occur at a conscious level are commonly referred to as self-control. Self-control has been defined as the capacity for resisting impulses and behaving in line with long-term goals or the social standards of the immediate situation (Baumeister, Muraven, & Tice, 2000).

Research by Baumeister and his colleagues suggests that we rely on a limited resource of mental energy that is expended when an individual engages in behaviors requiring self-control (Baumeister, Bratslavsky, Muraven, & Tice, 1998). Numerous studies have suggested that when this resource is depleted, it may lead to impaired performance on subsequent tasks that require self-control (e. g. , Baumeister, Heatherton, & Tice, 1994; Baumeister et al. , 1998, 2000; Muraven, Tice, & Baumeister, 1998). This phenomenon is commonly referred to as ego depletion (Baumeister, 2000).

Baumeister and his colleagues suggest that ego depletion is best understood using a strength model (Baumeister, Vohs, & Tice, 2007). In this model, the concept of self-control is frequently compared to a muscle in our body (Muraven & Baumeister, 2000). For example, just as muscles become tired after exertion, self-control diminishes after exertion as well. Numerous studies have found that when ego depletion occurs, our ability to subsequently focus on tasks that require active self-control is impaired (e. g. , Baumeister et al. , 1998; Muraven et al. , 1998; Schmeichel, Vohs, & Baumeister, 2003). Furthermore, Muraven and his colleagues found that the anticipation of future events requiring self-control influences individuals to conserve their energy on prior tasks that require self-control (Muraven, Shmueli, & Burkley, 2006). Finally, just as a tired boxer may exert more energy than he did during previous rounds when he knows that he can win the match if he beats his opponent in the final round, people tend to exert self-control despite ego depletion if there is enough incentive to do so. Muraven and Slessareva (2003), for example, found that the effects of ego depletion can be moderated on subsequent tasks requiring self-control if individuals perceive that there is enough incentive for the activity.

The studies reviewed above have all supported the idea that ego depletion can be understood using a strength model. Whereas these studies focus on how individuals use and conserve the resources necessary to engage in activities that require active self-control, other studies have examined the problematic implications of inadequate self-control. These studies discuss how low levels of self-control have been linked to a multitude of impulse-control problems, such as overeating, alcohol and drug abuse, crime and violence, overspending, sexually impulsive behavior, unwanted pregnancy, and smoking (e. g. , Baumeister et al. 1994; Baumeister, & Boone, 2004; Gottfredson & Hirschi 1990; Tangney, Baumeister, & Boone, 2004; Vohs & Faber, 2007). For example, Gottfredson and Hirschi (1990) advocated a theory of crime which assumes that the indispensable component of criminal behavior is a lack of self-control. Vohs and Faber (2007) found that participants who had been subjected to ego depleting activities experienced stronger urges to buy and were more likely to spend more money in unforeseen purchasing situations than individuals who were not experiencing ego depletion. Finally, Tangney et al. (2004) demonstrated in their study that a high level of self-control is correlated with better adjustment and positive relationships, higher grade point averages, less negative behaviors, and is also linked with emotional stability and conscientiousness when compared against individuals with low levels of self-control.

Based on the research findings described above, it is obvious that there are individual differences in our ability to engage in self-control. Past research has also indicated that there may be individual differences in how readily people deplete their limited resources when faced with situations requiring self-control. For example, Muraven and his colleagues found that individuals with a personality trait reflecting a higher temptation to drink alcohol consumed more alcohol after ego depletion compared to those lower in the personality trait (Muraven, Collins, & Nienhaus, 2002). Part of these differences seems to be caused by individual differences in our levels of self-control. These individual differences may be related to other commonly examined personality traits. The work of Tangney et al. (2004), for instance, suggests that individuals who are emotionally unstable have lower levels of self-control than individuals who are emotionally stable.

Clinical observations by Beck (1987) suggested that there are two personality dimensions related to emotional stability that influence one's vulnerability to depression; sociotropy and autonomy. Highly sociotropic individuals have a strong need for social acceptance and are often overly concerned with the possibility of being rejected by others. They will frequently behave in ways that they believe will please other people and are more likely to resort to seeking help from others in stressful situations (Beck, 1983, 1987). In other words, sociotropic individuals have a tendency to depend on acceptance and attention from others to become psychologically energized. Highly autonomous individuals, on the other hand, have an extreme need for independence and the accomplishment of personal goals. They may feel depressed or de-energized when they believe that they have failed and in an attempt to reduce this risk, they try to exert a great deal of control over their environment (Beck, 1983, 1987). Individuals who are high on either or both of these personality dimensions are at an increased risk of depression (Beck, 1983, 1987).

Furthermore, Beck (1987) suggested that individuals who are either highly sociotropic or highly autonomous are vulnerable to becoming depressed when faced with a threat or a loss in a domain corresponding to their specific type of individual investment. For example, a loss of a significant person in one's life may lead to depression and loss of energy in a sociotropic individual (Clark, Beck, & Brown, 1992; Hammen, Ellicott, Gitlin, & Jamieson 1989, 1992;

Kwon & Whisman, 1998; Robins & Block, 1988). On the other hand, repeated failure in the performance of personal tasks may be likely to lead to depression and loss of energy in an autonomous individual (Clark & Oates, 1995; Hammen et al. , 1989; Robins, Hayes, Block, Kramer, & Villena, 1995). This is commonly referred to as the stressor-vulnerability model of depression (Robins, 1990, 1995).

Robins (1995) suggested that depression can best be predicted not by knowledge of personality traits alone, nor solely by situational factors, but by the interactions between these two variables. This is consistent with Beck's (1987) stressor-vulnerability model of depression. It suggests that depression should be associated with specific congruent interactions between personality type and life event variables. For example, he hypothesized that depression should be associated with recent negative social events and a high level of sociotropy. Conversely, depression should also be associated with a high level of autonomy and recent negative autonomy related life events. While investigating this stressor-vulnerability model of depression, Robins found that highly depressed sociotropic patients reported more recent negative interpersonal life events than negative autonomy events and also reported more negative interpersonal events overall than did patients who were high in the personality dimension of autonomy (Robins, 1990). These findings support those of Beck (1987) which suggest that individuals high in the personality dimensions of sociotropy or autonomy are at an increased risk of depression and less emotionally stable than those low in these personality dimensions.

Drawing on the findings of Tangney et al. (2004) that individuals who are emotionally unstable have lower levels of self-control than those who are emotionally stable, as well as research which suggests that the personality dimensions of sociotropy and autonomy correlates negatively with emotional stability (Beck, 1987; Cappeliez, 1993; Dunkley, Blankstein, & Flett, 1997; Robins, 1990, 1995; Zuroff, 1994), this chapter presents the findings of two studies that investigated how highly sociotropic and autonomous individuals differ in their responses to the loss of this limited mental resource following tasks that require active self-control.

STUDY 1

Study 1 investigated whether, compared to individuals low in the personality dimensions of sociotropy and autonomy, highly sociotropic and autonomous individuals, respectively, have less mental energy to begin with and whether they expend more mental energy when they engage in tasks that require active self-control. Because highly sociotropic and autonomous individuals are at an increased risk of depression and are less emotionally stable than individuals low in this personality dimension (Beck, 1983, 1987; Robins, 1990, 1995), and because emotional instability is correlated with lower levels of self-control (Tangney et al. 2004), it was hypothesized that compared to individuals low in sociotropy or low in autonomy, highly sociotropic and autonomous individuals, respectively, would be more likely to persist less on difficult tasks in general as a result of having less mental energy to begin with. Additionally, compared to individuals low on these personality dimensions, highly sociotropic and autonomous people were expected to persist less on difficult tasks when experiencing ego depletion because we hypothesized that being emotionally unstable may make people expend greater mental energy when engaged in activities that require self-control.

Method

Participants

All participants were recruited from undergraduate psychology classes at a small liberal arts university in a rural area in the United States of America. These participants were informed that the research study was about "Personality and Taste Perception" and received a small amount of credit in their Psychology course for their participation. Eighty-nine participants (40 female & 39 male) participated in this study. The average age of the participants was 20. 7 (range: 18-33).

Materials

The research laboratory room was equipped with an electric oven and a refrigerator. Other equipment we used included a stopwatch, two identical bowls, a table, some chairs, a baking pan, a spatula, and numerous copies of a paper and pencil puzzle (explained in the Procedure section). We also prepared a few boxes of saltines and ready-made chocolate chip cookie dough that was stored in the refrigerator in the laboratory room.

To measure participants on the personality dimensions of sociotropy and autonomy, we used the Sociotropy-Autonomy Scale (Clark, Steer, Beck, & Ross, 1995). The Sociotropy-Autonomy Scale is a commonly used measure for assessing one's level of sociotropy and autonomy (Clark et al. , 1995;

Clark, Steer, Haslam, Beck, & Brown, 1997; Sato, 2003; Sato & McCann, 1997, 1998, 2000). This questionnaire consists of one scale for sociotropy and two scales for autonomy (Clark et al. , 1995). The sociotropy measure consists of twenty-eight items. The two autonomy scales are labeled: (1) solitude, and (2) independence. The solitude scale consists of thirteen items and the independence scale consists of seventeen items. Past research using the Sociotropy-Autonomy Scale has suggested that the "independence" measure is unrelated to vulnerability to depression (Bieling, Beck, & Brown, 2000; Clark et al. , 1995; Clark et al., 1997; Sato & McCann, 1997, 1998, 2002). Due to these findings, the present research will focus on the solitude scale as a measure for autonomy. The Sociotropy-Autonomy Scale requires participants to respond to each of the items on a five-point frequency scale from "never" to "all of the time". Scores are calculated separately for each of the three dimensions. All three measures have acceptable internal consistency (Cronbach alphas: Sociotropy. 87, Solitude. 70, Independence, 76) and temporal stability within 4-6 weeks (see Clark, et al., 1995).

Procedure

All participants were asked not to eat for two hours before their appointed time of participation in this research study. Individuals who reported that they had eaten within two hours of their appointed time were dismissed and asked to sign up again at another time. The remaining individuals who reported to the research laboratory at their appointed time were asked to read and sign an informed consent form. The laboratory had a table with two identical bowls. One bowl contained some chocolate chip cookies and the other contained some saltines. The researcher began baking chocolate chip cookies in the oven 5-10 minutes before each participant arrived. Therefore the laboratory smelled of freshly baked chocolate chip cookies.

After sitting in front of the two bowls at the table and signing the informed consent form, participants were asked to complete the Sociotropy-Autonomy Scale (Clark, Steer, Beck, & Ross, 1995). After completing this personality test, the participants were then asked to do one of two things depending on the experimental condition that they were randomly assigned to. For participants in the first condition (free choice condition), the researcher explained that she or he was investigating the effects of tasting two different types of food and asked the participants to make a choice as to whether they would like to eat two chocolate chip cookies or three saltines (the numbers are different because the one cookie was about 50% larger than one saltine). After they made their choice they were asked to eat the food they chose while the researcher was in the background filing some papers. Even though the researcher was not looking directly at the participant, she or he made sure that the participant ate only the food they chose and the correct quantity of it. The second group was considered to be the depletion condition. For participants in this condition, the experimenter gave the same explanations as the first group but added that although it was still his or her choice, the research team would appreciate it "very very very much" if the participant chose the saltines because there were too many people choosing the chocolate chip cookies. All participants in this group decided to cooperate and agreed to choose the saltines. After they made their choice they were asked to eat the saltines while the researcher was in the background filing some papers. As in the first group, even though the researcher was not looking directly at the participant, she or he made sure that the participant ate only the saltines and the correct quantity of it. Participants in both conditions were not permitted to drink liquids during the study. The second group was considered to be the depletion condition because it was assumed that choosing to eat the less attractive food and subsequently eating it in the presence of more attractive food requires a considerable amount of self-control.

After both groups consumed the food, they were informed that it was necessary to wait at least 20 minutes to allow the sensory memory of the food to fade. During this time, the researcher asked if the participants could participate in a "separate 20 minute study" that she or he was conducting. All participants agreed to participate in the "separate 20 minute study" and were provided with two puzzles to solve that required the person to trace a geometric figure without retracing any lines and without lifting his or her pen from the paper. The researcher gave two solvable practice problems as examples to help the participant understand the task. The researcher then provided the participant with two new puzzles and asked them to ring a bell when they had completed or wished to stop working on the puzzles. Participants were told they would be judged solely on whether or not they solved the puzzles. The experimenter then left the room and started a stopwatch hidden from the participant. Although the participants were not informed about this, these puzzles were unsolvable. We were only interested in examining the amount of time participants persisted on the puzzles until they stopped.

When the participant rang the bell, the experimenter stopped the stopwatch, entered the room, and fully debriefed the participant, clarifying to them that the puzzles were unsolvable. If the participant did not ring the bell after 20 minutes, the experimenter entered the room and fully debriefed the participant. Before they left, participants in the depletion condition were asked if they would have chosen the chocolate chip cookies if the researcher did not ask them to choose the saltines. Upon completion of this entire procedure, participants were debriefed and thanked for their participation. Participants were run one person at a time. Each session lasted approximately 30-45 minutes.

Results

The data of 22 participants were omitted from the analyses because of numerous reasons. Eight were omitted because the participant mistakenly thought that he or she solved the unsolvable puzzles. Seven were omitted because they chose the saltines instead of the chocolate chip cookies in the free choice condition and seven more were omitted because they stated that they would have chosen the saltines even if they were not asked to make that choice in the depletion condition. The individuals who chose or stated that they would have chosen the saltines instead of the chocolate chip cookies were asked why they made or would have made that choice. Most responded that they were either allergic to an ingredient in the cookie or were on a diet. The remaining sample used for the analyses consisted of 66 (24 male: 44 female) participants. The average age of the participants was 20. 6 (range: 18-33).

Two sets of analyses were conducted. First, the participants were divided into four groups based on two variables. For the first variable, participants were divided into groups of high and low sociotropy using a median split (median score = 58. 5). The second independent variable was the experimental conditions discussed in the Method section (free choice or depletion). The means and standard deviations for the number of seconds persisted on the puzzles for each group is listed in Table 1.

A 2 x 2 ANOVA revealed there was a significant difference between participants high in sociotropy and participants low in sociotropy in the time spent solving the puzzles $F(1,62) = 5. 21$, $p. < . 05$. Participants who were high in sociotropy spent less time solving the puzzles than did participants low in sociotropy. The main effect for experimental condition (free choice vs. saltine) was also significant $F(1,62) = 5. 96$, $p. < . 05$. Participants in the depletion condition spent less time solving the puzzles than those in the free choice condition. There was no significant interaction effect.

Table 1. Means and standard deviations of the number of seconds persisted on puzzles

Variable	Free Choice		Saltine	
	Mean	SD	Mean	SD
Hi Sociotropy	909. 57	325. 12	654. 83	309. 63
Lo Sociotropy	1006. 04	223. 01	897. 90	285. 23
Hi Autonomy	912. 19	326. 64	788. 73	374. 68
Lo Autonomy	1003. 65	222. 04	741. 91	263. 28

For the second set of analyses, the participants were divided into four groups based on two variables. For the first variable, participants were divided into groups of high and low autonomy (solitude) using a median split (median score = 17. 5). The second independent variable was the experimental conditions discussed in the Method section (free choice or saltines). A 2 x 2 ANOVA revealed a significant main effect for the experimental conditions $F(1,62) = 6. 34$, p. $< . 05$. Participants in the free choice condition persisted longer than participants in the depletion condition overall. There was no significant main effect for autonomy. Furthermore, the interaction effect was not significant. The means and standard deviations for the number of seconds persisted on the puzzles for each group is listed in Table 1. A graph of all of the means is also presented in Figure 1. One interesting finding about autonomy was that, even though we expected all participants with lower levels of autonomy to persist longer on the puzzles than individuals with high levels of autonomy, participants with high autonomy in the depletion condition persisted slightly longer on the puzzles than participants with low autonomy in the depletion condition (see Figure 1). Despite the fact that the interaction effect that corresponds to this unexpected finding turned out to be non-significant, it is nevertheless an interesting finding because individuals who are highly autonomous were expected to have less mental energy to engage in tasks that require self-control because they are considered to be emotionally unstable (Beck, 1987).

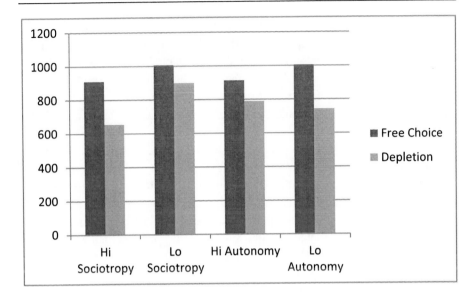

Figure 1. Means of the number of seconds persisted on puzzles.

Discussion

The less we have of this mental energy in reserve, the earlier we will deplete ourselves of this energy source when we engage in tasks requiring self-control. It was hypothesized that highly sociotropic participants would persist less on difficult tasks in general as a result of having less mental energy to begin with and this was indeed what was found. Although the findings of this study suggest that compared to individuals low in sociotropy, highly sociotropic individuals have less mental energy to begin with, it was not possible to conclude that they expend more mental energy when required to engage in active self-control. In spite of the fact that the difference in means between participants high and low in sociotropy is higher in the depletion condition than in the free choice condition, the interaction effect was not significant. The non-significance of the interaction effect may have been the result of the small sample size (N = 66) that was used in the present study and further research with larger samples may allow us to further examine the interaction between varying levels of sociotropy and active self-control.

The lower levels of energy available for self-control among highly sociotropic individuals may be one of the contributing factors in the etiology of sociotropic depression. The less we have of this mental energy in reserve, the more likely we will deplete ourselves of this energy source. Baumeister (2000) suggested that depletion of this form of mental energy corresponds to experiences of anxiety and depression. The findings of the present study suggest that examining how this form of energy is related to sociotropy and depression may have important theoretical implications in understanding the etiology of depression.

Contrary to our expectations, there was no significant main effect for autonomy. Furthermore, the interaction effect with the analyses for autonomy was not significant. Upon further examination of the data, we discovered that one of the reasons that the main effect for autonomy was non-significant was most likely caused by the fact that participants with high autonomy in the depletion condition persisted slightly longer on the puzzles than participants with low autonomy in the depletion condition (see Table 1). This finding was unexpected and surprising because, similar to sociotropy, individuals who are highly autonomous were expected to have less mental energy to engage in tasks that require self-control because they are considered to be more emotionally unstable (Beck, 1987). Despite the fact that the interaction effect that corresponds to this unexpected finding turned out to be non-significant, it may be possible that this would have been significant if we had a larger sample size.

This unexpected finding led us to the following speculation as to why this may have occurred. When we lose mental energy through self-control, we may become anxious or even depressed. Additionally, we become motivated to replenish the energy that we have lost. Highly sociotropic individuals may attempt to replenish their depleted mental energy by receiving social support through social interactions with other people. According to Beck (1983) highly sociotropic individuals tend to seek more help in general and may be more likely to resort to social interaction for both practical and emotional support when faced with stress. The unsolvable puzzles are stressful to participants and by giving up early, these individuals know that they can reengage in interpersonal interactions with important others sooner. These interactions may be a source of social support and thus a source of mental energy for these individuals. From this perspective, it seems reasonable that participants with high levels of sociotropy persisted less on the puzzles than individuals with low levels of sociotropy.

For highly autonomous individuals, however, this explanation may not apply. Highly autonomous individuals are more likely to replenish their depleted energy by successfully engaging in tasks that reflect positively on their sense of accomplishment. For these people, being depleted might motivate them to exert more effort into these tasks so that they are more likely to succeed in order to replenish their lost energy. Recent research suggests that there are indeed differences in personality that can influence how individuals attempt to replenish their mental energy that they have lost due to self-control (Sato, Harman, Donohoe, Weaver, & Hall, 2010). Further research examining how people with different personalities replenish lost mental energy may help us understand the nature of sociotropy and autonomy as well as treatment for these subtypes of depression.

STUDY 2

Beck (1983) suggested that both highly sociotropic and autonomous individuals are at an increased risk for depression. Furthermore, he suggested that even though highly sociotropic individuals attempt to replenish their depleted mental energy by receiving social support through social interactions with other people, individuals with high levels of autonomy tend to feel energized when they believe that they are skilled and accomplished at what they do (Beck, 1987). Study 2 examined how this loss of mental resources affects motivation for completing subsequent tasks reflecting personal accomplishments among individuals both high and low in sociotropy and autonomy. It was hypothesized that highly autonomous individuals would be more motivated to perform well on tasks that reflect their personal skills and accomplishments than individuals low in autonomy. Moreover, because highly autonomous individuals heavily invest in their personal skills, when energy is lost due to tasks requiring high levels of self-control, these individuals would perceive succeeding at a personal task as a way to regain energy they have lost. Therefore, they would be more motivated to perform well on subsequent tasks compared to individuals low in autonomy as well as highly autonomous individuals who were initially not subjected to tasks requiring a high level of self-control. It was also hypothesized that, because sociotropic individuals do not have the tendency to replenish their lost energy by succeeding in personal tasks reflecting their sense of accomplishment, engaging in tasks that require self-control may not increase their motivation to perform well on subsequent personal tasks. If there is an effect, we expect that the task requiring self-control will lower motivation on subsequent tasks due to ego depletion.

Method

Participants

All participants were recruited from undergraduate psychology classes at a small liberal arts university in a rural area in the United States of America. These participants were informed that the research study was about "Personality and Task Performance" and received a small amount of credit in their Psychology course for their participation. A total of 139 individuals (58 males, 81 females) volunteered, reported to the research laboratory during their appointed time, and participated in the study. The mean age of the participants of this sample was 19. 9 (range = 18-44).

Materials

The research laboratory room was equipped with a stopwatch, photocopied pages from an old textbook in Psychology, a laminated sheet of paper with a 6 x 6 matrix of letters, and some paper and pencils. To measure participants on the personality dimensions of sociotropy and autonomy, we used the Sociotropy-Autonomy Scale (Clark et al. , 1995). The Sociotropy-Autonomy Scale is the personality test that was used in Study 1 (see Method section in Study 1 for details).

Procedure

Participants were asked to report to a research laboratory and sign an informed consent form. After providing informed consent by signing the form, they were asked to complete the Sociotropy-Autonomy scale (Clark et al. , 1995). Participants were randomly divided into two groups, the "easy" group and the "depletion" group.

Participants in the easy group were provided with two photocopied 8. 5" by 11" pages from a classic textbook on Personality Psychology (Kluckhohn, Murray, & Schneider, 1953). The content of the pages, "National Character" was chosen for its irrelevance to the present study. These participants in the easy group were asked to cross out all of the letter "e"s in the pages provided. They were asked to start from the beginning of the first page and continue as quickly as possible and complete as much as they could in 5 minutes. Participants in the depletion group were provided with much lighter photocopies of the same pages as the first group so that the pages were more difficult to read. They were then asked to cross out all of the letter "e"s that are neither adjacent to another vowel nor one letter away from another vowel in the same word. Thus the participants in the second group did not cross out the letter "e" in the word "vowel" even though the participants in the first group id. The participants in the second group were also asked to start from the beginning of the first page and continue as quickly as possible. They were told that they had, "5 minutes to complete the task". Due to the demanding nature of the task for this depletion group compared to the task of the easy group, this group was considered to expend more mental energy that is required for self-control. For participants in both groups, the experimenter left the lab immediately after the participant began the task and started a stopwatch. The experimenter confirmed that the participants were engaged in the task through a one-way mirror. After five minutes, the experimenter re-entered the lab and asked the participant to stop the task. The experimenter then collected the photocopied pages that the participant worked on.

After the participants completed this task, the researchers provided the participants with a word find task using a 6 x 6 matrix of letters for participants to solve. The task required the participant to find as many English words with three letters or more using consecutive letters in the matrix. No proper names or slang were to be used. They were allowed to go horizontally, vertically, and diagonally in both ways. They were also able to change directions in the middle of the word. They were not allowed to return to the same letter in the same location in the matrix when forming one word. They were asked to write down as many words as they could find on a separate sheet of lined paper. For every three-lettered word, the participant received one point. For every four-lettered word, the participant receives two points. For every five-lettered word, the participant receives three points. This point system continues on for six, seven, etc. lettered words. The longer the word, the more points they received. The experimenter provided the instructions and explained the point system to the participant and informed the participants that they had three minutes to complete the task. The experimenter measured the 3 minutes using a stopwatch and asked the participant to stop at the three-minute mark. The matrix and the lined sheet were then collected by the experimenter. The participants were then debriefed and thanked for their participation. The experimenters then calculated the scores of each participant on the word find task making sure that each word that was reported was a possible solution using the matrix and recorded this information for each participant. Participants were run one individual at a time. Each session lasted approximately 20-30 minutes.

Results

The data of ten participants were not included in the analyses because of incomplete data. Eight participants misunderstood the directions for the first part of the study (crossing out "e"s) and two participants did not respond to all of the questions on the Sociotropy-Autonomy scale (Clark et al, 1995). The remaining sample consisted of 129 (53 males, 76 females) participants. The mean age of the participants of this sample was 20. 0 (range = 18-44).

Two sets of analyses were conducted. First, the participants were divided into four groups based on two variables. The first independent variable was determined by the experimental conditions discussed in the Method section (easy or depletion). For the second variable, participants were divided into groups of high and low autonomy (solitude) using a tertiary split (scores < 16. 3 & > 21. 0). Participants who had a score between 16. 3 and 21. 0 were omitted from the analyses because they were considered to be neither high nor low in autonomy. Thus the sample used for this set of analyses consisted of 94 participants (57 female, 37 male) and the mean age was 20. 2 (range = 18-44). The reason why a tertiary split was used in this study instead of a median split (as was used in Study 1) was because scatterplots of the word find scores revealed that individuals with autonomy scores in the middle 33% range varied without any identifiable pattern even after dividing participants into their experimental conditions (easy or depletion). However, when their scores were examined in relation to their experimental conditions, there was a clearly identifiable difference in word find scores between the individuals in the top 33% and bottom 33% in their autonomy scores. The means and standard deviations for the scores on the word find task are listed in Table 2.

A 2 x 2 ANOVA using these two variables revealed that there was a significant main effect for autonomy levels (high autonomy vs. low autonomy) $F(1, 93) = 162. 646$, $p < . 001$. As expected, participants high in autonomy scored higher on the word-find task than participants low in autonomy. The main effect for the experimental condition (easy vs. depletion) was also significant $F (1, 93) = 17. 820$, $p < . 001$. Participants in the depletion group scored higher in the word-find task than the participants in the easy group. There was also a significant interaction effect between experimental condition (easy vs. depletion) and autonomy levels (high autonomy vs. low autonomy) $F (1, 93) = 31. 283$, $p < . 001$. As expected, a Tukey's post hoc test of means revealed that although there was no difference in the word-find scores between the easy group and the depletion group for participants low in autonomy, high autonomy participants in the depletion group (M = 34. 42) scored higher on the word-find task than high autonomy participants in easy task group (M = 23. 80; see Figure 2).

**Table 2. Means and standard deviations for the scores
of the word-find task**

Variable	Easy		Depletion	
	Means	SD	Means	SD
Hi Sociotropy	21. 38	6. 45	23. 48	10. 04
Lo Sociotropy	23. 50	7. 69	22. 52	11. 01
Hi Autonomy	23. 80	4. 10	34. 42	7. 39
Lo Autonomy	16. 05	4. 92	14. 56	3. 17

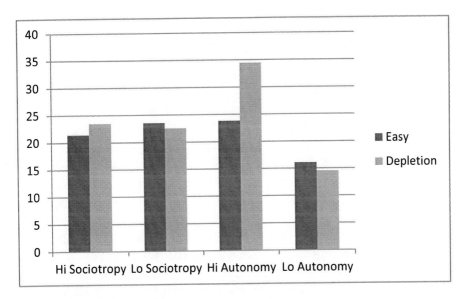

Figure 2. Means for the scores of the word-find task.

For the second set of analyses, the participants were divided into four groups based on two variables. The first independent variable was the experimental conditions discussed in the Method section (easy or depletion).

For the second variable, participants were divided into groups of high and low sociotropy using a tertiary split (scores < 56. 3 & > 69. 0). We used a tertiary split for this set of analyses to stay consistent with the analyses for autonomy in this study. Participants who had a score between 56. 3 and 69. 0 were omitted from the analyses because they were considered to be neither high nor low in autonomy. Thus the sample used for this set of analyses consisted of 90 participants (54 female, 36 male) and the mean age was 20. 1 (range = 18-44). The mean and standard deviations for the scores on the word find task are listed in Table 2. A 2 x 2 ANOVA using these two variables revealed that there were no significant main effects. The interaction effect was also found to be non-significant. A graph of all of the means for both analyses is presented in Figure 2.

Discussion

Study 2 investigated how the loss of mental energy as a result of an ego-depleting task would affect the motivation of individuals high in sociotropy and autonomy compared to those low in these personality traits. The results of the study revealed two very interesting findings. The first was that highly autonomous individuals have more motivation to perform well on personal tasks requiring self-control than individuals low in autonomy in general. The other finding that was of great interest was that highly autonomous individuals' motivation to perform well on personal tasks increases more than those low in autonomy following a task that requires active self-control.

The hypothesis that individuals high in the personality dimension of autonomy would be more motivated to perform well on tasks that reflect their personal skills and would lead to feelings of personal accomplishment than those low in autonomy was supported. Participants high in autonomy scored significantly higher on the word-find task than participants low in autonomy. This result was unsurprising, given that in contrast to highly sociotropic individuals or people low in autonomy, highly autonomous individuals tend to feel more energized when they believe that they are skilled at something or that they have succeeded at a personal task (Beck, 1987).

Additionally, the results supported our hypothesis that highly autonomous individuals will be more motivated to perform well when energy is lost due to prior tasks requiring active self-control compared to participants low in autonomy and those high in autonomy who have not experienced an ego-depleting activity. Highly autonomous participants in the depletion condition scored significantly higher on the word-find task than highly autonomous participants in the easy group. Because highly autonomous individuals tend to place greater emphasis on personal accomplishments and may feel de-energized and depressed when they believe that they have failed, succeeding at a personal task may viewed as a method of regaining the lost mental energy from a prior task requiring active self-control. Thus, highly autonomous individuals may be more motivated to perform well on subsequent tasks that lead them to feel as though they have demonstrated their skills or made a personal accomplishment in an effort to regain their lost mental energy or to protect themselves from feeling depressed.

In contrast to our interesting findings regarding autonomy, the analysis for sociotropic participants was non-significant. This could be due to the fact that sociotropic individuals are not motivated to replenish their lost energy by succeeding in personal tasks or gaining a sense of accomplishment. Therefore, engaging in tasks that require active self-control will not increase their motivation to perform well on subsequent personal tasks. We had hypothesized that engaging in tasks that require active self-control might lead to lower motivation for these individuals to perform well on subsequent tasks, but our findings did not support this. A further explanation of our non-significant findings in regards to sociotropy could be that the task that we utilized as an ego depletion task did not cause ego depletion in highly sociotropic individuals. The task that was assumed to cause ego depletion in this study was the activity of crossing out the e's in the lightly copied pages of text. This is quite unrelated to social support or interpersonal relationships, which are of primary concern to highly sociotropic individuals. Thus, it is possible that, compared to individuals high in autonomy, having to focus on a task of crossing out e's in a text would not deplete the mental resources of individuals high in sociotropy as much. In the future, it may be useful to explore the possibility of using a task in the social domain which would cause more ego depletion among highly sociotropic individuals.

GENERAL DISCUSSION

The studies summarized in the chapter thus far examined how highly sociotropic or autonomous individuals differ in their response to the loss of mental energy following tasks that require active self-control. The combined results of both studies suggest that individuals high in these respective personality dimensions do differ in their performance following loss of mental energy as a result of engaging in tasks that require self-control.

Study 1 specifically investigated whether individuals high in sociotropy or autonomy have less mental energy to begin with. Additionally, this experiment examined whether they expend more mental energy when they engage in tasks that require self-control than those low in the respective personality dimensions. Because individuals high in sociotropy or autonomy are generally less emotionally stable than those low in these personality dimensions (Beck, 1983, 1987) and because emotional instability has been correlated with lower levels of self-control (Tangney et al., 2004), it was hypothesized highly sociotropic or autonomous individuals would be more likely to give up earlier on subsequent tasks following ego-depleting activities as a result of having less mental energy to begin with. Furthermore, it was predicted that individuals high in these personality dimensions would persist less on the difficult tasks when experiencing ego depletion because being emotionally unstable may cause people to expend greater mental energy when engaging in activities that require self-control.

The results of Study 1 revealed that overall, highly sociotropic individuals persisted less than those low in sociotropy. In spite of the fact that the differences in means between participants high and low in sociotropy is higher in the treatment condition that was considered to cause ego depletion, than in the control (free choice) group, the interaction effect was not significant. Thus, although the findings suggest that compared to individuals low in sociotropy, highly sociotropic individuals have less mental energy to begin with, it was not possible to conclude that they expend more mental energy when required to engage in active self-regulation. It was suggested that the non-significance of the interaction effect may have been the result of the small sample size that was used in Study 1 and future research with larger samples of subjects may permit us to examine the interaction between different levels of sociotropy and active self-control more closely.

Contrary to our hypotheses, there was no significant main effect for autonomy and the interaction effect was also not significant. This finding was unexpected because, similar to highly sociotropic individuals, people high in autonomy were expected to have less mental energy to begin with and also to expend more mental energy when required to engage in self-regulating tasks. Neither of these hypotheses were supported by the results of Study 1, although it is possible that significant results would have been found with a larger sample size.

The results of Study 1 suggesting that highly sociotropic individuals persist less when experiencing ego depletion than those low in that personality trait was unsurprising. The results in regards to autonomy, however, were unexpected. When individuals lose mental energy, they may become depressed or anxious and may also become motivated to replenish this lost energy in some manner. Because of the high emphasis that highly sociotropic individuals place on their relationships with others, it may be reasonable to speculate that they would be more likely to attempt to regain lost mental energy through interpersonal interactions. Because the achievement of a personal accomplishment, such as solving the puzzle in Study 1, would not help a highly sociotropic individual regain lost mental energy, they would not be motivated to persist on working on the puzzle for long, especially when they are experiencing ego depletion. Experiencing ego depletion may actually have the opposite effect on highly sociotropic individuals in regards to persistence on such personal tasks. Because social interactions with peers may be viewed as a method of regaining lost mental energy, highly sociotropic individuals may be motivated to persist less on subsequent problem solving tasks in an effort to leave the experiment and engage in social interactions with others.

Highly autonomous individuals, in comparison to highly sociotropic individuals, value the accomplishment of personal goals over social interactions with their peers and thus, are potentially more motivated to persist longer on puzzles when experiencing ego depletion. Past work by Sato et al. (2010) has suggested that when highly autonomous individuals have depleted their mental energy, they may seek the achievement of personal goals as a method of regaining these resources.

Regardless of the possible reasons why we found these interesting results in Study 1, these findings have important theoretical implications. Lower levels of mental energy available for self-regulation among highly sociotropic individuals may be one of the contributing factors to sociotropic depression. The less mental energy that an individual has to begin with, the more likely he or she will deplete those resources, potentially resulting in depression. Additionally, the findings of Study 1 suggest that research examining the different ways in which highly sociotropic and autonomous individuals seek to replenish lost mental energy is necessary. Although these notions regarding how ego depletion influences the motivation of sociotropic and autonomous individuals were entertained as a result of Study 1, they were merely speculations. Study 2 was designed to examine how ego depletion influences these individuals' motivations in a more direct fashion.

In Study 2, it was hypothesized that highly autonomous individuals would be more motivated to perform well on tasks that reflect their personal skills than those low in autonomy. Furthermore, as suggested from the results of Study 1, because highly autonomous individual invest a great deal in their personal accomplishments, when mental energy is lost due to tasks that require high levels of self-control, these individuals are likely to perceive succeeding at a personal task as a method of regaining lost mental energy. Thus, highly autonomous individuals were expected to be more motivated to perform well on subsequent personal tasks following ego-depleting activities than those low in autonomy as well as highly autonomous individuals who were initially not subjected to tasks requiring a high level of self-control. It was further hypothesized that because sociotropic individuals do not perceive the accomplishment of personal goals as a method of regaining lost mental resources, engaging in tasks that require self-control would not increase their motivation to perform well on subsequent personal tasks. It was expected that if there was any effect at all in regards to sociotropic individuals, it would be that ego-depleting activities would lower their motivation to perform well on subsequent tasks.

The results of Study 2 revealed two very interesting findings. The first interesting finding supported the hypothesis that highly autonomous individuals have more motivation to perform well on personal tasks that require active self-control than individuals low in autonomy overall. The second interesting result also confirmed the hypothesis that highly autonomous individuals' motivation to perform well on subsequent personal tasks increased more than those low in autonomy following an ego-depleting task. Finally, the hypothesis that experiencing ego depletion would not lead to higher motivation to perform personal tasks in highly sociotropic individuals was supported, as the analysis of the results in regards to sociotropic individuals was non-significant.

The results of Study 2 were unsurprising, given that highly autonomous individuals place great emphasis on the achievement of personal goals while highly sociotropic individuals do not. Because individuals experiencing ego depletion often attempt to replenish their lost mental resources, it is not surprising that highly autonomous individuals would seek to regain lost resources through the achievement of personal goals, which would energize them, causing them to be more motivated to perform well on subsequent personal tasks. Conversely, because demonstrating personal skills and accomplishing personal goals would not make highly sociotropic individuals feel energized and would be an unlikely way in which these individuals would seek to regain lost mental resources, the fact that experiencing ego depletion did not motivate highly sociotropic individuals to perform well on the subsequent personal task was an expected finding.

We had hypothesized in Study 2 that if significant results were found for highly sociotropic individuals, it would be that experiencing ego depletion would lead to lower motivation for these individuals to perform well on subsequent personal tasks, but this hypothesis was not supported. The non-significant results found in Study 2 in regards to highly sociotropic individuals may have been the result of a small sample size. Furthermore, the non-significant results could be explained by the fact that the task that was used as an ego-depleting activity did not lead to ego depletion in highly sociotropic individuals. Because the ego-depleting activity was unrelated to interpersonal relationships which are of immense concern to highly sociotropic individuals, it is possible that in contrast to those high in autonomy, not performing well on the ego-depleting task did not deplete the mental resources of individuals high in sociotropy. A potential avenue for future research could be focused on developing appropriate tasks in the social sphere which would cause ego depletion in highly sociotropic individuals.

If our interpretations of the findings of Study 2 are accurate, these discoveries could have practical implications for therapy in depressed individuals. Depressed, highly autonomous individuals may benefit by consulting with therapists to help find personal tasks at which they are likely to succeed. In contrast, highly sociotropic individuals could work with therapists in an effort to enhance their satisfaction with their interpersonal relationships. While our research suggests that succeeding at personal tasks may be viewed as a method of replenishing lost mental resources among individuals high in autonomy, future research focusing on ways in which highly sociotropic individuals replenish their lost mental energy (perhaps through social interactions with others) is needed. Furthermore, exploring subsequent avenues for long term treatment of depression and recuperation of mental energy in both highly autonomous and highly sociotropic individuals may have very useful practical implications in the future.

If the interpretations we have suggested for the findings of Study 1 and Study 2 are accurate, they would suggest that highly sociotropic and autonomous individuals differ in their motivation to perform following tasks that require self-control. The findings of Study 1 suggests that highly sociotropic individuals may have less of the limited mental resource required to engage in self-control than those low in sociotropy. The results of Study 2 suggest that experiencing ego depletion may lead to increased motivation to perform well on subsequent personal tasks for individuals high in autonomy compared to those low in autonomy and to individuals high in autonomy who have not depleted their mental resources. The results also suggest that ego depletion will not lead to increased motivation to perform well on personal tasks among highly sociotropic individuals, probably because the accomplishment of personal goals is not perceived as an important method of regaining lost mental energy for highly sociotropic individuals.

The studies summarized above are not without limitations. For example, both studies examined data from small sample sizes and it is possible that more significant results would have been found had the experiments been conducted on larger samples. Additionally, the subjects used in both experiments were a sample of college students and did not examine individuals from clinical populations. Investigating the differences between clinically depressed individuals who are highly sociotropic or autonomous might lead to a deeper understanding of how long term treatment of depression could be tailored to fit the individual needs of people based on whether they are highly sociotropic or autonomous. Finally, it is possible that the ego-depleting activity used in Study 2 did not result in ego depletion for highly sociotropic individuals which could potentially explain the non-significant findings in regards to sociotropy in that study. Because highly sociotropic individuals are far more concerned with their interpersonal relationships with others, it is unlikely that focusing on a personal task requiring self-control would lead to ego depletion in these individuals to the same extent that it would in highly autonomous individuals.

Future research studies should focus on larger, clinical populations because the results of the studies summarized above suggest that research into the differences between highly sociotropic and autonomous individuals in regards to how these individuals deplete and subsequently replenish mental resources could undoubtedly have not only important theoretical but also practical implications for the treatment of clinical depression. Nevertheless, we hope that the two studies presented here will serve as an important step in the process of making new discoveries in this direction.

ACKNOWLEDGMENTS

The authors would like to thank Catherine E. Beer, Laura Leady, Toni Torquato, Lauren Hoke and Miles Lyons for their tireless efforts to help collect data for this study.

REFERENCES

Baumeister, R. F. (2000). Ego depletion and the self's executive function. In A. Tesser, R. B. Felson, & J. M. Suls (Eds.) *Psychological perspectives on self and identity*, (pp. 9-33). Washington, DC: American Psychological Association.

Baumeister, R. F. , Bratslavsky, E. , Muraven, M. & Tice, D. M. (1998). Ego depletion: Is the active self a limited resource? *Journal of Personality and Social Psychology, 74*, 1252-1265.

Baumeister, R. F. , Heatherton, T. F. , & Tice, D. M. (1994). *Losing control: How and why people fail at self-regulation.* San Diego, CA: Academic Press.

Baumeister, R. F. , Muraven, M. & Tice, D. M. (2000). Ego depletion: A resource model of volition, self-regulation, and controlled processing. *Social Cognition, 18*, 130-150.

Baumeister, R. F. , Vohs, K. D. , & Tice, D. M. (2007). The strength model of self-control. *Current Directions in Psychological Science, 16,* 351-355.

Beck, A. T. (1983). Cognitive therapy of depression: New perspectives. In P. J. Clayton & J. E. Barrett (Eds.) *Treatment of depression: Old controversies and new approaches*, (pp. 265-290). New York: Raven Press.

Beck, A. T. (1987). Cognitive models of depression. *Journal of Cognitive Psychotherapy, An International Quarterly, 1*, 5-37.

Bieling, P. J. , Beck, A. T. , & Brown, G. K. (2000). The sociotropy-autonomy scale: Structure and implications. *Cognitive Therapy and Research, 24,* 763-780.

Cappeliez, P. (1993). The relationship between Beck's concept of sociotropy and autonomy and the NEO-Personality Inventory. *British Journal of Clinical Psychology, 32,* 78-80.

Clark, D. A. , Beck, A. T. , & Brown, G. K. (1992). Sociotropy, Autonomy, and life event perceptions in dysphoric and nondysphoric individuals. *Cognitive Therapy and Research, 16*, 635-652.

Clark, D. A. , & Oates, T. (1995). Daily hassles, major and minor life events, and their interaction with sociotropy and autonomy. *Behaviour Research and Therapy, 33,*819-823.

Clark, D. A. , Steer, R. A. , Beck, A. T. , & Ross, L. (1995). Psychometric characteristics of revised sociotropy and autonomy scales in college students. *Behaviour Research and Therapy, 33,* 325-334.

Clark, D. A. , Steer, R. A. , Haslam, N. , Beck, A. T. , & Brown, G. K. (1997). Personality vulnerability, psychiatric diagnoses, and symptoms: Cluster analyses of sociotropy autonomy subscales. *Cognitive Therapy and Research, 21,* 267-283.

Dunkley, D. M. , Blankstein, K. R. , & Flett, G. L. (1997). Specific cognitive-personality vulnerability styles in depression and the five-factor model of personality. *Personality and Individual Differences, 23,* 1041-1053.

Gottfredson, M. R. , & Hirschi, T. (1990). *A general theory of crime.* Palo Alto, CA: Stanford University Press.

Hammen, C. , Ellicott, A. , & Gitlin, M. (1992). Stressors and sociotropy/autonomy: A longitudinal study of their relationship to the course of bipolar disorder. *Cognitive Therapy and Research, 16,* 409-418.

Hammen, C. , Ellicott, A. , Gitlin, M. , & Jamieson, K. R. (1989) Sociotropy/autonomy and vulnerability to specific life events in patients with unipolar depression and bipolar disorders. *Journal of Abnormal Psychology, 98,* 154-160.

Kluckhohn, C. , Murray, H. A. , & Schneider, D. M. (Eds.). (1953). *Personality in nature, society, and culture* (2nd ed.). New York: Knopf.

Kwon, P. , & Whisman, M. A. (1998). Sociotropy and autonomy as vulnerabilities to specific life events: Issues in life event categorization. *Cognitive Therapy and Research, 22,* 353-362.

Muraven, M. , & Baumeister, R. F. (2000). Self-regulation and depletion of limited resources: Does self-control resemble a muscle? *Psychological Bulletin, 126,* 247-259.

Muraven, M. , Collins, R. L. , & Nienhaus, K. (2002). Self-control and alcohol restraint: An initial application of the self-control strength model. *Psychology of Addictive Behaviors, 16,* 113-120.

Muraven, M. , Shmueli, D. , & Burkley, E. (2006). Conserving self-control strength. *Journal of Personality and Social Psychology, 91,* 524-537.

Muraven, M. , & Slessareva, E. (2003). Mechanisms of self-control failure: Motivation and limited resources. *Personality and Social Psychology Bulletin, 29,* 894-906.

Muraven, M. , Tice, D. M. , & Baumeister R. F. (1998). Self-control as limited resource: Regulatory depletion patterns. *Journal of Personality and Social Psychology, 74,* 774-789.

Robins, C. J. (1990). Congruence of personality and life events in depression. *Journal of Abnormal Psychology, 99,* 393-397.

Robins, C. J. (1995). Personality-event interaction models of depression. *European Journal of Personality, 9,* 367-378.

Robins, C. J. , & Block, P. (1988). Personal vulnerability, life events, and depressive symptoms: A test of a specific interaction model. *Journal of Personality and Social Psychology, 54,* 847-852.

Robins, C. J. , Hayes, A. M. , Block, P. , Kramer, R. J. , & Villena, M. (1995). Interpersonal and achievement concerns and the depressive vulnerability and symptom specificity hypothesis: A prospective study. *Cognitive Therapy and Research, 19,* 1-20.

Sato, T. (2003). Sociotropy and autonomy: The nature of vulnerability. *The Journal of Psychology, 137,* 447-466.

Sato, T. , & McCann, D. (1997). Vulnerability factors in depression: The facets of Sociotropy and Autonomy. *Journal of Psychopathology and Behavioral Assessment, 19,* 41-62.

Sato, T. , & McCann, D. (1998). Individual differences in relatedness and individuality: An exploration of two constructs. *Personality and Individual Differences, 24,* 847-859.

Sato, T. , & McCann, D. (2000). Sociotropy-autonomy and the Beck Depression Inventory. *European Journal of Psychological Assessment, 16,* 66-76.

Sato, T. , & McCann, D. (2002). Advances in the study of sociotropy-autonomy and depression. In S. P. Shohov (Ed.), *Advances in psychological research* (Vol. 17, pp. 35-53). Hauppage, New York: Nova Science.

Sato, T. , Harman, B. A. , Donohoe, W. M. , Weaver, A. , & Hall, W. A. (2010). Individual differences in ego depletion: The role of sociotropy-autonomy. *Motivation and Emotion, 34,* 205-213.

Schmeichel, B. J. , Vohs, K. D. , & Baumeister, R. F. (2003). Intellectual performance and ego depletion: Role of the self in logical reasoning and other information processing. *Journal of Personality and Social Psychology, 85,* 33-46.

Tangney, J. , Baumeister, R. , & Boone, A. (2004). High self-control predicts good adjustment, less pathology, better grades, and interpersonal success. *Journal of Personality, 72,* 271-322.

Vohs, K. , & Faber, R. (2007). Spent resources: Self-regulatory resource availability affects impulse buying. *Journal of Consumer Research, 33,* 537-547.

Zuroff, D. C. (1994). Depressive personality styles and the five-factor model of personality. *Journal of Personality Assessment, 63,* 453-472.

In: Psychology of Self-Control
Editors: A. Durante, et. al.

ISBN: 978-1-61470-881-0
© 2012 Nova Science Publishers, Inc.

Chapter4

A COMPUTERIZED DETOUR TASK FOR THE ASSESSMENT OF SELF-CONTROL BEHAVIOR

Theodore A. Evans and *Michael J. Beran*

Language Research Center
Georgia State University
University Plaza
P. O. Box 5010, Atlanta, GA, U. S.

Abstract

The detour task is a classic problem in which a participant must ascertain how to obtain a reward item that is placed on the opposite side of a barrier. A direct response to the reward is typically not possible and must be inhibited. Instead, the participant must move away from the reward in order to detour the barrier and ultimately gain access to the reward. Many species have proved capable of solving variations of the task, albeit in different ways and at different speeds. We created a novel variation of this task for presentation on a computer monitor, building upon the strengths of the original detour problem and other previous tests of self-control behavior. In two experiments, nine rhesus monkeys (*Macacamulatta*) had to detour a cursor around a bar-shaped stimulus that represented a small reward in order to reach a more distant stimulus that

---

* E-mail address: theodore. evans@gmail. com

represented a large reward. In Experiment 1, monkeys' performance on this variation of the task was compared to a more traditional self-control test in which monkeys chose to move a cursor one of two durations/distances to select stimuli representing different size rewards. In the traditional test, all monkeys were heavily biased to the self-control (larger-further) response, whereas monkeys' performance in the detour test was more variable and positively related to age and/or experience. Older monkeys with more computerized test experience were more often willing to detour the small reward stimulus to select the large reward stimulus. In Experiment 2, we eliminated the latter relationship by training less experienced monkeys to accurately move the cursor around a non-reward barrier. Following this training, all nine monkeys were retested in the computerized detour task and all were biased to make the detour response or were indifferent between the two response options. These results indicate that this computerized detour task provides a novel assessment of self-control behavior, different from that of the traditional self-control test. Further research is needed with these and other tasks to elucidate what specific task requirements result in differential performance like that seen in the present study.

Keywords: Detour, self-control, computerized testing, rhesus monkey.

There has been a resurgence of interest in the long-standing topic of self-control in nonhuman animals (Rachlin, 2000). This interest is driven by the recognition that lack of inhibitory control may cause difficulties in other behaviors, more so than those difficulties being the result of perceptual or cognitive limitations. Executive functions such as working memory, controlled attention shifting, metacognition, prospective memory, and planning all may rely to varying degrees on behavioral inhibition and the ability to inhibit prepotent responses in service of obtaining later, better outcomes (e. g. , Posner & Rothbart, 1998, 2000; Shamosh et al. , 2008).

Early work in the area of self-control in animals was focused on discrete choice tasks where animals chose between two outcomes, one of which involved a more immediate, but smaller or less preferred reward, and the other involved a delayed, but larger or more preferred outcome. Although animals often made impulsive responses, limiting their maximization of reward, a number of tests showed self-control abilities in rats, pigeons, and monkeys (Ainslie, 1974; Grosch& Neuringer, 1981; Logue, 1988; Mazur, 2000;

Rachlin, 2000; Tobin, Chelonis, & Logue, 1993; Tobin, Logue, Chelonis, Ackerman, & May, 1996). Subsequent studies used different methods requiring inhibitory control, such as the reverse-reward paradigm in which the smaller or less preferred item must be selected for the larger or more preferred item to be obtained (Boysen& Berntson, 1995). Although not all species can successfully negotiate the different versions of this task that have been used, many succeed given the right level of training or the right experimental designs (e. g. , Albaich-Serrano, Guillén-Salazar, & Call, 2007; Boysen, Berntson, Hannan, & Cacioppo, 1996; Boysen, Mukobi, & Berntson, 1999; Genty& Roeder, 2007; Kralik, 2005; Murray, Kralik, & Wise, 2005; Silberberg & Fujita, 1996; Vlamings, Uher, & Call, 2006).

Tests of delay of gratification initially developed for children (e. g. , Metcalfe & Mischel, 1999; Mischel, Shoda, & Rodriguez, 1989; Toner & Smith, 1977) also have been modified for use with animals (e. g. , Beran, Savage-Rumbaugh, Pate, & Rumbaugh, 1999). In one of these tests, first given to great apes (Beran, 2002), animals had to sustain their self-control by continually avoiding the impulsive response of taking and eating less preferred or smaller amounts of food. Although some species showed only limited delay of gratification in this paradigm (e. g. , Vick, Bovet, & Anderson, 2010), others are more successful. For example, when food accumulated within reach, as long as none was eaten, apes showed high levels of self-control by delaying their gratification (Beran, 2002; Beran & Evans, 2006, 2009), and they even showed strategic responses such as self-distraction to facilitate longer delay (Evans & Beran, 2007a), although monkeys tested to date have been less successful (Anderson, Kuroshima& Fujita, 2010; Evans & Beran, 2007b).

Another inhibition task that has been presented in various forms to nonhuman animals is the detour task (Köhler, 1925). This task originally was presented in a naturalistic setting, where a food item was placed behind a barrier and animals had to go around the barrier to reach the food rather than moving directly to the food. Many species proved capable of solving variations of the task, albeit in different ways and at different speeds (e. g. , chimpanzees: Köhler 1925; Kellog& Kellog, 1933; chicks: Regolin, Vallortigara, & Zanforlin, 1995; cats: Poucet, Thinus-Blanc & Chapuis, 1983; dogs: Pongracz, Miklosi, Kubinyi, Gurobi, Topal, & Csanyi, 2001; quails, gulls, & canaries: Zucca, Antonelli, & Vallortigara, 2005; mosquitofish: Bisazza, Pignatti, & Vallortigara, 1997). This task provided evidence of comparative differences in inhibitory control, as only through inhibiting a tendency to move directly toward food could animals succeed.

Recently, this task has been presented on a smaller spatial scale, with various puzzle boxes that allow reward items to be placed in clear containers for which access can only be gained through an indirect reach into the container. The idea here is that inhibition of the prepotent tendency to reach directly towards the reward is necessary for a subject to be able to gain the reward. This task has been given to a number of species, including human children, with mixed results. Diamond (1981) found that 7- to 9-month-old human infants had trouble solving the task. Diamond and Goldman-Rakic (1986) reported that adult rhesus monkeys solved the test, but 2- to 4-month-old monkeys and adult monkeys with lesions of the dorsolateral prefrontal cortex did not succeed. Santos, Ericson, and Hauser (1999) reported that tamarins had difficulty solving the task when a transparent box was presented (and the food was visible) but not when the box was opaque. Marmosets also succeeded with the task even with transparent boxes, unless they had damage to their orbitofrontal lobe, in which case they required training with opaque boxes before they could succeed (Wallis, Dias, Robins, & Roberts, 2001). Capuchin monkeys succeeded immediately in the task, showing that some species apparently have better control over prepotent response inhibition (Lakshminarayanan & Santos, 2009). Great apes also succeeded in the task, sometimes even outperforming 3- to 5-year old children (Vlamings, Hare, & Call, 2010).

The detour problem is particularly useful because it can be presented in so many different ways. We adapted the test for presentation on a computer monitor, and we built upon the strengths of the detour problem and other previous tests of self-control behavior. In our version of the problem, rhesus monkeys (*Macacamulatta*) were trained that each of two unique visual stimuli led to different numbers of food rewards. Sometimes, the stimulus that led to more food reward was the closer stimulus to a cursor on the screen, but other times it required the monkey to move the cursor longer and farther to obtain the larger reward. In addition, the monkey sometimes had to move the cursor around the small-reward stimulus in order to make contact with the large-reward stimulus. Unlike the manual detour task, where a non-edible, physical barrier was between the subject and the reward, in our task that barrier actually provided reward, albeit a smaller amount. Thus, monkeys had to choose to pursue the larger reward amount, and then sustain that choice as they approached and moved around the stimulus that would have provided an immediate, smaller reward. In some regards, the inhibition resembles that of some other computer tasks used with animals, such as maze tasks where the animal must move away from the goal to actually reach it (Fragaszy, Johnson-

Pynn, Hirsh, & Brakke, 2003; Miyata & Fujita, 2008; Washburn, Hopkins, & Rumbaugh, 1991; Washburn & Rumbaugh, 1992), but it also offers the novel opportunity for the monkeys to change their response at any time and take the smaller reward. Thus, the task required the same inhibitory responses of the detour task, but required a component of sustained self-control that is novel for a computerized task and that also is distinguishable from the manual detour task.

With this task, we assessed two hypotheses. The first was that rhesus monkeys would succeed in this new paradigm by detouring the small reward stimulus to reach the large reward stimulus in a significant proportion (> 50%) of trials. This is based on previous work with this species on other tasks of inhibition and self-control, including the accumulating reward delay of gratification task adapted from research with children to be used with great apes (Beran, 2002; Beran & Evans, 2006). Although not nearly as successful as chimpanzees, rhesus monkeys have shown the ability to wait for some accumulating items before consuming any of such items (Evans & Beran, 2007b). Rhesus monkeys also have exhibited success in a computerized test of delayed gratification, in which they made repeated choices between working to earn future rewards and receiving previously earned rewards (Evans, 2007). One reason that rhesus monkeys may exhibit self-control (as opposed to impulsivity) in such tasks is that they are despotic and nepotistic primates, and so they may be suited to avoiding nearby resources, particularly while in the presence of dominant conspecifics in order to avoid conflict with those individuals.

Despite our expectation that rhesus monkeys would exhibit self-control in the computerized detour task, our second hypothesis was that monkeys would show less self-control in this task relative to a more traditional smaller-sooner vs. larger-later self-control test. This is because this new computerized detour task combines components of other previously established tests, potentially making the new test more difficult than the others. Monkeys had to choose between two differentially delayed rewards, in addition to continually inhibiting a response to the small reward stimulus as it was by-passed by the cursor. The more traditional self-control test only requires the first component (delay choice), and is thus less likely to tax monkeys' self-control capacity relative to the new computerized detour task.

EXPERIMENT 1

Methods

Participants. We tested nine male rhesus monkeys: Obi (age 6), Han (age 7), Luke (age 10), Chewie (age 10), Murph (age 16), Lou (age 16), Willie (age 24), Gale (age 26), and Hank (age 26). Monkeys were individually housed with constant visual and auditory access to other monkeys. All monkeys had 24-hour access to water, as well as frequent access to computerized testing systems, from which they could earn banana flavored grain-based food pellets. All monkeys were fed manufactured chow and various fruits and vegetables daily between 1600 and 1800 hours.

Five monkeys (Gale, Hank, Lou, Murph and Willie) were previously tested in a computerized discrete-choice self-control task (Beran, unpublished data), and four monkeys (Chewie, Gale, Luke and Obi) were previously tested in a computerized delay maintenance task (Evans, 2007). Additionally, all monkeys were previously tested in a non-computerized delay maintenance task (Evans & Beran, 2007b).

Design and Procedure. All monkeys were tested using the Language Research Center's Computerized Test System (Richardson, Washburn, Hopkins, Savage-Rumbaugh, & Rumbaugh, 1990). This system allowed monkeys to manipulate a joystick (*Logitech*, Fremont, CA) to control a cursor on a computer monitor and thereby respond to various digital stimuli. The computer rewarded correct responses with 94-mg banana-flavored pellets (*Bio-Serv*, Frenchtown, NJ) using a dispenser interfaced to the computer through a digital I/O board (*Keithley Instruments*, Cleveland, OH).

The computerized task was a variation of a delay-discounting test, in which monkeys chose between a small reward amount and a large reward amount, each delivered after a different delay interval. In all trials, the small reward amount consisted of one fruit-flavored pellet and was represented by a light-blue thin rectangular stimulus with black cross-hatching. The large reward amount consisted of four fruit-flavored pellets, and was represented by a red thin rectangular stimulus with a vertical line pattern. The delays that preceded reward delivery were determined by the distance between the cursor and each stimulus on the 27 cm^2 test screen at the beginning of the trial (i. e. , the farther the cursor was from the stimulus, the longer it would take the monkey to use the cursor to select that stimulus). These delays/distances varied between experimental conditions. Distance (both digital and actual) has been used successfully as a determinant of self-control in previous investigations with nonhuman animals (Evans, 2007; Evans & Westergaard, 2006; Stevens, Rosatti, Ross & Hauser, 2005), and so we believed that it would be appropriate for the current study.

All trials within a session had a fixed duration of 30 sec, timed from the beginning of one trial to the beginning of the next. A start-screen preceded each trial, in which monkeys initiated the trial by moving the cursor into contact with a square stimulus positioned in the center of the computer screen. The reward stimuli then appeared on the screen and the trial timer began. At the end of the 30 sec trial interval, any ongoing trial activity was cancelled, and the start-screen reappeared. Monkeys initiated and completed as few or as many trials as they so chose until the end of a session. Sessions occurred once daily for a maximum of 4 hours, and session start times varied from day to day.

All test sessions began with a block of forced trials in which only one of the two reward stimuli appeared on the computer screen with the cursor. In each of these trials, the cursor was positioned in the center of the screen and an 18 cm long stimulus was positioned 2 cm from one of the four screen edges (determined randomly at the beginning of each trial). A 3-second response duration was required to contact the stimulus. Monkeys completed 10 pairs of forced trials, in which the small-reward trial and the large-reward trial (within each pair) were ordered randomly. This trial block provided monkeys with an opportunity to learn about (or be reminded of) the amount of reward that was associated with each stimulus before they were required to choose between those stimuli in later test trials.

Next in the session was a block of 20 trials in which the monkeys chose between a small-reward stimulus and a large-reward stimulus, each 18 cm in length and positioned on opposite edges of the computer screen (either left/right or top/bottom, determined randomly). Because the cursor was positioned in the center of the screen, the choice options in this trial block were always equidistant from the cursor, and a 3-second response duration was required to select either stimulus. Monkeys' performance in trials of this block (hereafter referred to as centered trials) provided a baseline measure of their preference for the small and large reward stimuli.

The remainder of each session consisted of test trials. We presented two test trial types in this experiment to assess whether monkeys would avoid selecting a nearby small-reward stimulus in order to select a more distant large-reward stimulus. We conducted two separate phases of test sessions each consisting of a unique test trial type (see below). Thus, in each session of each phase, monkeys completed a block of forced trials, a block of centered trials, and then as many phase-appropriate test trials as they so chose until the end of the session. We continued to present each monkey with the same test phase until the monkey completed three consecutive sessions with stable preference levels for the two reward stimuli (in the test trials only), at which point we presented the monkey with the next phase. We considered preference levels to be stable when the monkey's selections of small and large reward stimuli differed by no more than 20% across the 3 sessions.

Phase 1: Baseline Self-Control. The first type of test trials served as a baseline measure of monkeys' self-control in this paradigm. These trials assessed the influence of cursor proximity to the small-reward stimulus (i. e. , the impulsive choice option) at the start of the trial on monkeys' self-control. These trials were similar to centered trials with the exception that the cursor began in 1 of 5 possible positions between the two reward stimuli (Figure 1a). The five locations were equally spaced between the two stimuli and thus could be 4 cm from either stimulus, 8 cm from either stimulus, or halfway between the two stimuli (12 cm from either stimulus). Contacting the large-reward stimulus from these distances required response durations of 1, 2, 3, 4, and 5 seconds. Trials were presented in 5-trial blocks with each cursor position occurring once in random order within each block.

Phase 2: Detour Self-Control. The second trial type tested whether having to maneuver the cursor around the impulsive choice option would decrease monkeys' self-control more than simply having to move away from it. In those trials, one 18-cm-long reward stimulus was positioned along one of the four screen edges, as in a forced trial (hereafter referred to as the far stimulus). The other reward stimulus was positioned in the middle of the computer screen (hereafter referred to as the near stimulus), parallel to the far stimulus, and varied in length (3 cm, 9 cm, or 18 cm). This created 6 unique trial types, because either the small-reward stimulus or the large-reward stimulus could occupy the near or far stimulus position (Figure 1b). The cursor was always positioned 4 cm from the center of the near stimulus, and always on the opposite side of the near stimulus from the far stimulus. Trials were presented in 6-trial blocks with each trial type occurring once in random order within each block. Contacting the near stimulus directly in any of these trials required a 2-second response duration, whereas detouring the near stimulus and contacting the far stimulus required minimum response durations of 4, 5, and 6 seconds, depending on the size of the near stimulus.

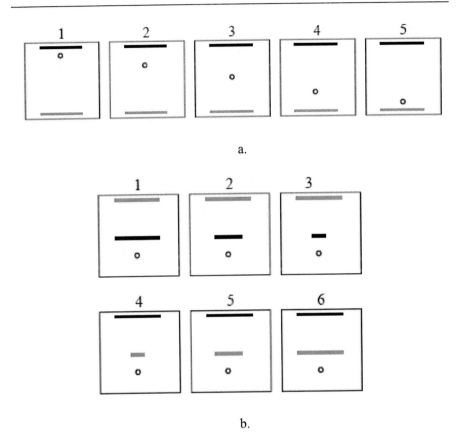

a.

b.

Figure 1. Versions of the computerized task presented to monkeys in Experiment 1-Phase 1 (a), Phase 2 (b). Within each phase, trial types are numbered from least to most taxing with regard to self-control. Black and gray lines represent large- and small-reward stimuli, respectfully.

Results

In both phases, all monkeys completed 100% of forced trials and centered trials within the allotted time. Also, in both phases, monkeys selected the large-reward stimulus in 100% of centered trials. Further, in both phases, monkeys continued to participate in test trials following the forced and centered trial blocks, and they completed 96-100% of test trials within the allotted time.

Phase 1: Baseline Self-Control. In completed trials, the monkeys chose the large-reward stimulus in nearly 100% of trials. This occurred regardless of whether the cursor's starting position was 4, 8, 12, 16, or 20 cm from the large-reward stimulus (Means, respectively: 100%, 99. 88%, 100%, 99. 88% and 99. 55%).

Phase 2: Detour Self-Control. Monkeys' stimulus selections were more variable than in Phase 1. Only when the large-reward stimulus occupied the near stimulus position did monkeys consistently select that stimulus, and they did so whether it was 18 cm, 9 cm, or 3 cm in length (Means, respectively: 100%, 100% and 99. 63).

However, when the small-reward stimulus occupied the near stimulus position (i. e. , when some measure of self-control was required because monkeys had to go around the small-reward stimulus to get to the large-reward stimulus), monkeys' responses were more variable (see Figure 2). A single factor (center stimulus length) repeated measures ANOVA revealed an effect of near-stimulus length on percent selection of the large-reward stimulus (self-control), $F(1, 8) = 4. 123$, $p = 0. 036$, $\eta_p^2 = 0. 340$. Monkeys exhibited fewer self-control responses for longer near stimuli (see Figure 2).

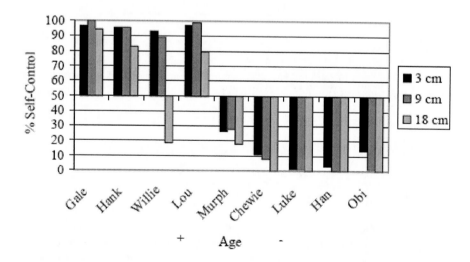

Figure 2. Rhesus monkey performance in critical trials of Experiment 1-Phase 2. In these trials, a rectangular small-reward stimulus occupied the center of the screen. Bar height/direction represents the percentage of self-control (large-reward stimulus) responses. Bar color represents the length of the small-reward stimulus.

Additionally, self-control in each of these three trial types was positively related to age, $r = 0.77$ to 0.90, n = 9, all $p < 0.05$. The oldest four individuals each exhibited a 79-100% bias to the self-control response in two or three trial types, while the youngest four individuals exhibited an 86-100% bias to the impulsive (small-reward) response.

Discussion

Monkeys exhibited no difficulty in avoiding the small-reward stimulus when the cursor was positioned anywhere between the two response options on the test screen. Thus, monkeys of both species clearly preferred to spend more time in order to obtain a greater reward when time was the only variable differentiating the response options. However, when faced with circumventing the small-reward stimulus to obtain a larger reward, monkeys exhibited a greater level of impulsivity. The less direct the route was to the large reward, the less likely monkeys were to complete the detour and obtain the larger reward.

Importantly, the amount of time required to select the large reward stimulus was comparable across the two test phases of this experiment, even though one phase allowed for a direct route to the large reward stimulus and the other did not. Particularly, in the highest two levels of Phase 1 and the lowest two levels of Phase 2, a minimum of 4 or 5 seconds was required to obtain the larger reward. Because monkeys exhibited relatively fewer large-reward responses in the Phase 2 levels, in which they had to inhibit a direct response to the nearest reward stimulus, in addition to having to spend a similar amount of time making the large reward response as in Phase 1, the detour component of the Phase 2 task was most likely responsible for the difference in performance.

Although all monkeys nearly always selected the large-reward stimulus when it occupied the near stimulus position, the youngest monkeys reversed their response preference to the more direct option when a variable-length small-reward stimulus occupied the center of the screen. The older monkeys maintained an overall preference for the self-control option, but not to the degree exhibited when the large-reward stimulus occupied the near stimulus position. These findings suggest that rhesus monkeys' capacity for self-control develops with age and/or experience into adulthood.

However, there was one factor that co-varied with age and species in this study, and that was computer-task experience. Although all animals had several years of experience solving psychological tasks in the computerized format, there was variability in exactly how many years and in how many studies each monkey had participated. As noted above, older cohorts of monkeys had relatively more computerized testing experience, and so, it is difficult to separate years of maturation from years of computerized testing experience for this colony. Given the close relationship between these three variables, we designed a second experiment to disentangle potential experience-based differences in computer task performance from age-based differences in self-control performance.

EXPERIMENT 2

If differences in computerized testing experience could explain the pattern of results exhibited in Experiment 1, a likely cause would be differential precision in motor control of the cursor via the joystick. This is because less precise control of the cursor while attempting to circumvent the small-reward stimulus could result in inadvertent selection of the small-reward stimulus, and could therefore reduce the frequency of self-control responses. For this reason, the goal of this experiment was to train the monkeys to precisely detour a non-reward stimulus and then examine the effect of this training on their performance in the self-control detour task. Successful training in the non-reward detour task would equate monkeys on this dimension of computerized testing experience and therefore would remove this covariate from the experiment.

Methods

Participants. We tested the same nine monkeys that were tested in Experiment 1.

Design and Procedure. We used the same computerized test apparatus as in Experiment 1. The task consisted of four distinct phases that were presented sequentially and automatically within a session by the computerized test system. Progression through the tasks was dependent on performance: monkeys had to make the correct or preferred response (see below for details) in 16 of 20 consecutive trials in a particular phase to be successful. Each monkey was presented with this automated series of phases until it advanced to the final test phase in either three consecutive sessions or three of four consecutive sessions.

Monkeys were presented with two different versions of this automated task. We first presented each monkey with a version in which the detour stimuli were 9 cm in length. In Experiment 1, younger/less experienced monkeys all exhibited at least a partial bias to the impulsive response in trials involving center stimuli of this length. Once a particular monkey succeeded on the 9-cm task version (as described above), we presented a version involving 18-cm detour stimuli. In Experiment 1, almost all younger/less experienced monkeys showed a complete bias for the impulsive response in trials involving center stimuli of this length.

Phase 1: S⁺/S⁻ Discrimination. The first phase of the automated task consisted of a two-choice discrimination task involving side-by-side 9-cm rectangular stimuli presented along one of the four edges of the screen (see Figure 3). Screen edge was selected at random by the program. The cursor was presented near the opposite screen edge, 20 cm from the pair of stimuli, and therefore required a minimum of 5 seconds to reach either stimulus. The S^+ was solid yellow and contacting it with the cursor resulted in the delivery of a single food pellet and a 5 sec inter-trial interval consisting of a blank screen. The S^- was white with black cross-hatching and contacting it with the cursor resulted in the repositioning of the cursor to its trial-start location. To progress from one trial to the next, monkeys had to select the S^+ (i. e. , monkeys could select the S^- an infinite number of times in a single trial before selecting the S^+). Thus, a successful trial in this phase was defined as selection of the S^+ in the first response of the trial. This phase ensured that monkeys knew which of two stimuli provided reward and which did not.

Phase 2: S⁺/S⁻ Detour. The second phase consisted of a detour task involving the S^+ and S^- stimuli from Phase 1. At the start of each trial, the S^- occupied the screen-center position and, depending on the task version, was either 9 cm or 18 cm in length (See Figure 3). The S^+ was always positioned near the opposite edge of the computer screen as the cursor and was always 18 cm in length. The response contingencies from Phase 1 remained in place for Phase 2. Thus, the monkey had to detour the cursor around the S^- in order to contact the S^+ and receive a reward. As in Experiment 1, this detour response required a minimum of 5 or 6 seconds, depending of the center stimulus length. The same performance criterion was used to determine success as in the previous phase. This phase ensured that each monkey could move the cursor around one stimulus to make contact with another one, and here there was no requirement for self-control because only one stimulus resulted in reward.

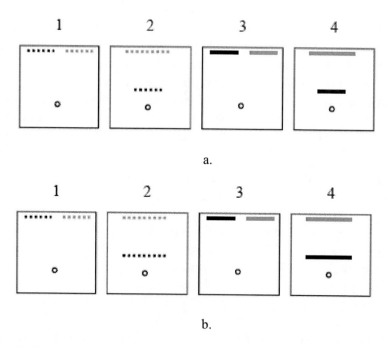

Figure 3. Versions of the computerized task presented to monkeys in Experiment 2- Phase 1 (a), Phase 2 (b). Within each phase, trial types are numbered in the order in which they were presented within a session. Dashed black and gray lines represent S⁺ and S⁻ stimuli, respectfully, whereas solid black and gray lines represent large-reward and small-reward stimuli, respectively.

Phase 3: Large Reward/Small Reward Discrimination. This phase was similar to the two-choice discrimination task of Phase 1. However, instead of involving an S⁺/S⁻ pair, this task involved the choice between side-by-side large- and small-reward stimuli (see Figure 3c). These stimuli looked exactly as they did in Experiment 1, and selection of each was followed by the same response contingencies (delivery of either four or one food pellets). One other difference between this phase and previous phases is that each trial's duration was 30 sec, regardless of the monkey's selection (after a selection was made, all on-screen elements disappeared and the screen remained blank for the remainder of the trial duration). Therefore, a successful trial was one in which the large reward stimulus was selected within the 30-sec trial duration. This phase reminded the monkeys of the two reward contingencies and re-instilled the basic outcomes of the self-control test.

Phase 4: Detour Self-Control. The final phase was the test phase and it was very similar to the test trials of Experiment 1. Fifty percent of these trials were experimental trials in which an 18-cm large-reward stimulus was centered along one of the four screen edges, the cursor was positioned near the opposite screen edge, and the small-reward stimulus (9 cm or 18 cm in length, depending on the task version) was positioned halfway between the cursor and the large-reward stimulus (hereafter referred to as experimental trials; see Figure 3d). The remaining trials were control trials in which the positions of the large- and small-reward stimuli were reversed. Monkeys were presented with test trials for the remainder of their computer session. Now, it was empirically confirmed that monkeys could move around one stimulus to get to another (Phase 2), and the question was whether they would chose to do so in this self-control task.

Results

In the 9-cm version of the task, all tested monkeys advanced through all four task phases and completed the required number of sessions involving Phase 4 test trials. Monkeys required a mean of 6. 43 sessions to succeed in the 9-cm task version. In the 18-cm version of the task, all tested monkeys except for one advanced through all four task phases. Obi (age 7) did not advance beyond Phase 2 in any of the 30 sessions in which he worked on the task. The remaining monkeys required a mean of 13. 0 sessions to complete the experiment.

In Phase 4 control trials (in which the large-reward stimulus occupied the screen-center position), all monkeys selected the large-reward stimulus in 100% of trials in both the 9-cm and 18-cm task versions. In Phase 4 experimental trials (in which the small-reward stimulus occupied the screen-center position), large-reward (i. e. , self-control) responses were less frequent (52-100%; see Figure 4). A single factor repeated measures ANOVA revealed no effect of center stimulus length on percent selection of the large-reward stimulus (i. e. , self-control), $F(1, 12) = 2. 509, p = 0. 139$. Further, there was no relationship between self-control and age in either task version:9 cm: $r = 0. 647$, n = 9, $p = 0. 06$; 18 cm: $r = 0. 621$, n = 8, $p = 0. 100$.

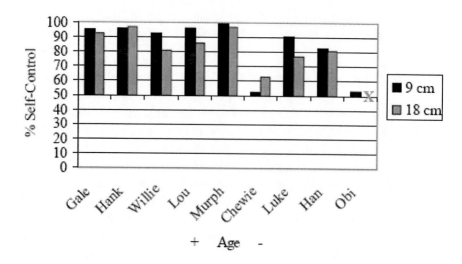

Figure 4. Rhesus monkey performance in critical trials of Experiment 2-Phase 4. In these trials, a rectangular small-reward stimulus occupied the center of the screen. Bar height represents the percentage of self-control (large-reward stimulus) responses. Bar color represents the length of the small-reward stimulus. An "x" in place of a bar indicates that the monkey did not complete the relevant phase of the experiment.

Discussion

We designed this experiment to eliminate one alternative explanation for the age related differences in self-control performance exhibited in Experiment 1, namely differential ability to precisely control the digital cursor (as a result of differential experience with the computerized testing environment). The automated task that we created for this purpose successfully trained all monkeys to detour at least a medium-length nearby stimulus and contact a distant stimulus in order to receive a reward. However, the task did not necessarily train monkeys to detour all center stimuli, as monkeys continued to select the large-reward stimulus whenever it occupied the central position. Further, the task did not simply train the monkeys to produce more self-control responses, as monkeys still exhibited a wide range of preference for the two possible responses. Most importantly, the age-related difference in behavior seen in these same rhesus monkeys in the previous experiment did not carry over to this one.

GENERAL DISCUSSION

The overall goal of this study was to demonstrate the value of the computerized detour self-control task by presenting it to a colony of computer-trained rhesus monkeys and evaluating their performance. We assessed two hypotheses regarding the monkeys' performance of this task. The first was that rhesus monkeys would exhibit self-control in this new paradigm by detouring the small reward stimulus to reach the large reward stimulus in a significant proportion (> 50%) of trials. We found considerable evidence to support this hypothesis. In Experiment 1, four monkeys exhibited a substantial (80-100%) bias to the self-control response in at least two of the three critical task versions (Figure 2). Further, in Experiment 2, monkeys that were previously biased to impulsivity (showing 0-30% self-control responses), exhibited a substantially larger portion (50-100%) of responses in favor of self-control (Figure 4).

We predicted that rhesus monkeys would be able to perform this task because of their performance in previously conducted self-control studies, as well as due to aspects of their social behavior. Rhesus monkeys have exhibited varying degrees of success in delay discounting, delay of gratification, and manual detour experiments (e. g. Anderson & Woolverton, 2003; Diamond & Goldman-Rakic, 1986; Evans, 2007; Evans & Beran, 2007b; Santos et al. , 1999; Szalda-Petree, Craft, Martin, & Deditius-Island, 2004). Additionally, rhesus monkeys are characterized as highly despotic and nepotistic primates, and this may have promoted greater self-control in their evolutionary history. There is a clear advantage to avoiding preferred resources until more dominant individuals have passed them by, and such avoidance may even involve physically detouring around such resources. Of course, more tests need to be conducted with this species in different social environments to confirm such a possibility.

Despite our expectation that rhesus monkeys would exhibit success in the computerized detour task, our second hypothesis was that monkeys would show less self-control in this task relative to a more traditional smaller-sooner vs. larger-later self-control test. In the case of the latter test, all monkeys almost exclusively (in 99-100% of trials) performed the self-control response when their cursor began somewhere between the two reward stimuli, and monkeys had only to decide whether moving the cursor the required duration/distance to the large reward stimulus was worth the added reward amount. As mentioned above, in the computerized detour test, monkeys exhibited a larger range of performance. However, even individuals that were biased to self-control in both experiments made fewer self-control responses in the detour task in comparison to the more traditional self-control test.

The difference in performance between the detour self-control task and the traditional self-control task most likely reflected the difference in self-control requirements between those tasks. The more traditional self-control test only required monkeys to make an isolated choice between the smaller/sooner/closer reward stimulus and the larger/later/farther reward stimulus. This was similar to the dichotomous choices presented to rhesus monkeys in previously conducted temporal discounting tasks (Anderson & Woolverton, 2003; Szalda-Petree et al., 2004). However, the detour self-control test required additional self-control beyond this initial choice between differentially delayed rewards. Monkeys were further taxed with the repeated opportunity to overturn their initial choice as they moved their cursor closer to the small reward stimulus along the path to the large reward stimulus. This element of sustained self-control has rarely been assessed in laboratory tests with nonhuman animals and only in isolation of the more common discrete self-control choice. In one previous test, rhesus monkeys exhibited some ability to sustain self-control by refraining from eating an accumulating pile of reward items for several seconds and occasionally for more than a minute (Evans & Beran, 2007b).

While there were some potential alternative explanations for this performance difference, none of them were supported by the data. For instance, the difference in performance between task types could not have been the result of purely temporally based decision making. Both task types required similar minimum response durations to obtain the larger reward,even though one phase allowed for a direct route to the large reward stimulus and the other did not. The amount of time required to select the large reward stimulus in the two task types overlapped at the 4-5 second range, and monkeys performed differentially on the two tasks despite the similar temporal parameters. Further, this performance difference could not be explained by the order in which the tasks were presented, as monkeys showed higher self-control performance in the task presented first (smaller-sooner vs. larger-later task) than in the task presented second (detour task). Additionally, monkeys' performance could not be linked to the amount of experience they had with each task type, because monkeys were given significantly more experience in the latter task (in which they exhibited relatively less self-control), in the interest of improving younger/less experienced monkeys' performance in that task.

This new task provided some interesting differences in performance across these monkeys. Given the overall success of rhesus monkeys on the manual reaching detour task (e. g., Diamond & Goldman-Rakic, 1986; Santos et al. , 1999), we hoped that the current task would provide a greater challenge, and it did. In the process of making it more challenging, we changed the nature of the task so that it required more than one self-control component. The involvement of both delay choice and sustained self-control made this computer task unique and may make it a good model for self-control decisions in natural situations. Some of the most taxing self-control situations are those in which one must choose forego something that is immediately compelling for something that is more valuable long-term, and then maintain that decision until the delayed reward is received. For example, opting to save one's extra income for a big purchase rather than spending it right away, and then inhibiting future temptations to spend those accumulating savings on frivolous items requires such maintained self-control. Natural examples for nonhuman animals would most certainly be on a more limited temporal scale, but could still involve the same basic elements. For example, an animal may decide to engage in tool-use to obtain a rare and nutritionally dense food source rather than forage for generally available small bits of food, and then persist in such behavior even when lower-effort, yet lower value, resources are available throughout the time-course of a successful bout of tool behavior. Future investigations of self-control behavior may benefit by attempting to correlate the existence of such natural examples of both discrete and sustained behavioral components, with laboratory models of self-control behavior like the computerized detour self-control task.

ACKNOWLEDGMENTS

This research project was supported by grants HD-38051 and HD-060563 from the National Institute of Child Health and Human Development and grant BCS-0924811 from the National Science Foundation.

REFERENCES

Ainslie, G. W. (1974). Impulse control in pigeons. *Journal of the Experimental Analysis of Behavior, 21*, 485-489. doi: 10. 1901/jeab. 1974. 21-485.

Amici, F. , Aureli, F. & Call, J. (2008). Fission-fusion dynamics, behavioral flexibility, and inhibitory control in primates. *Current Biology, 18*, 1415-1419. doi: 10. 1016/j. cub. 2008. 08. 020.

Anderson, J. R. , Kuroshima, H. , & Fujita, K. (2010). Delay of gratification in capuchin monkeys (*Cebus apella*) and squirrel monkeys (*Saimirisciureus*). *Journal of Comparative Psychology, 124*, 205-210. doi: 10. 1037/a0018240.

Anderson, K. G. , & Woolverton, W. L. (2003). Effects of dose and infusion delay on cocaine self-administration choice in rhesus monkeys. *Psychopharmacology, 167*, 424-430.

Beran, M. J. (2002). Maintenance of self-imposed delay of gratification by four chimpanzees (*Pan troglodytes*) and an orangutan (*Pongopygmaeus*). *Journal of General Psychology, 129*, 49-66. doi: 10. 1080/00221300209602032.

Beran, M. J. , & Evans, T. A. (2006). Maintenance of delay of gratification by four chimpanzees (*Pan troglodytes*): The effects of delayed reward visibility, experimenter presence, and extended delay intervals. *Behavioural Processes, 73*, 315-324. doi: 10. 1016/j. beproc. 2006. 07. 005.

Beran, M. J. , & Evans, T. A. (2009). Delay of gratification by chimpanzees (*Pan troglodytes*) in working and waiting situations. *Behavioural Processes, 80*, 117-121. doi: 10. 1016/j. beproc. 2008. 11. 008.

Beran, M. J. , Savage-Rumbaugh, E. S. , Pate, J. L. , & Rumbaugh, D. M. (1999). Delay of gratification in chimpanzees (*Pan troglodytes*). *Developmental Psychobiology, 34*, 119-127. doi:10. 1002/(SICI)1098-2302(199903)34:2<119::AID-DEV5>3. 0. CO;2-P.

Bisazza, A. , Pignatti, R. , & Vallortigara, G. (1997). Laterality in detour behaviour: Interspecific variation in poeciliid fish. *Animal Behaviour, 54*, 1273–1281. doi: 10. 1006/anbe. 1997. 0522.

Boysen, S. T. , & Berntson, G. G. (1995). Responses to quantity: Perceptual versus cognitive mechanisms in chimpanzees (*Pan troglodytes*). *Journal of Experimental Psychology: Animal Behavior Processes, 21*, 82-86. doi: 10. 1037/0097-7403. 21. 1. 82.

Boysen, S. T. , Berntson, G. G. , Hannan, M. B. , & Cacioppo, J. T. (1996). Quantity-based interference and symbolic representations in chimpanzees (*Pan troglodytes*). *Journal of Experimental Psychology: Animal Behavior Processes, 22*, 76-86. doi: 10. 1037/0097-7403. 22. 1. 76.

Boysen, S. T. , Mukobi, K. L. , & Berntson, G. G. (1999). Overcoming response bias using symbolic representations of number by chimpanzees (*Pan troglodytes*). *Animal Learning and Behavior, 27*, 229-235. doi: 10. 1037/0735-7036. 115. 1. 106.

Diamond, A. (1981). Retrieval of an object from an open box: The development of visual-tactile control of reaching in the first year of life. *Society of Research in Child Development Abstracts, 3*, 78.

Diamond, A. , & Goldman-Rakic, P. S. (1986). Comparative development in human infants and infant rhesus monkeys of cognitive functions that depend on prefrontal cortex. *Neuroscience Abstracts, 12*, 742.

Evans, T. A. (2007). Performance in a computerized self-control task by rhesus macaques (*Macacamulatta*): The combined influence of effort and delay. *Learning and Motivation, 38*, 342-357. doi: 10. 1016/j. lmot. 2007. 02. 001.

Evans, T. A. , & Beran, M. J. (2007a). Chimpanzees use self-distraction to cope with impulsivity. *Biology Letters, 3*, 599-602. doi: 10. 1098/rsbl. 2007. 0399.

Evans, T. A. , & Beran, M. J. (2007b). Delay of gratification and delay maintenance by rhesus macaques (*Macacamulatta*). *Journal of General Psychology,134*, 199-216. doi: 10. 3200/GENP. 134. 2. 199-216.

Evans, T. A. & Westergaard, G. (2006). Self-control and tool-use in tufted capuchin monkeys (Cebus apella). *Journal of Comparative Psychology, 120*, 163-166. doi:10. 1037/0735-7036. 120. 2. 163.

Fragaszy, D. , Johnson-Pynn, J. , Hirsh, E. , & Brakke, K. (2003). Strategic navigation of two-dimensional alley mazes: Comparing capuchin monkeys and chimpanzees. *Animal Cognition, 6,* 149-160. doi: 10. 1007/s10071-002-0137-8.

Genty, E. , & Roeder, J. J. (2007). Transfer of control in black (*Eulemurmacaco*) and brown (*Eulemurfulvus*) lemurs: Choice of a less preferred food item under a reverse-reward contingency. *Journal of Comparative Psychology, 121*, 354-362. doi: 10. 1037/0735-7036. 121. 4. 354.

Grosch, J. , & Neuringer, A. (1981). Self-control in pigeons under the Mischel paradigm. *Journal of the Experimental Analysis of Behavior, 35*, 3-21. doi: 10. 1901/jeab. 1981. 35-3.

Kellogg, W. N. & Kellogg, L. A. (1933). *The ape and the child.* New York: Hafner Publishing Co.

Köhler, W. (1925). *The mentality of apes.* London: Routledge and Kegan Paul.

Kralik, J. D. (2005). Inhibitory control and response selection in problem solving: How cotton-top tamarins (*Saguinasoedipus*) overcome a bias for selecting the larger quantity of food. *Journal of Comparative Psychology, 119*, 78-89. doi: 10. 1037/0735-7036. 119. 1. 78.

Lakshminarayanan, V. R. , & Santos, L. R. (2009). Cognitive preconditions for responses to fairness: An object retrieval test of inhibitory control in capuchin monkeys (*Cebus apella*) *Journal of Neuroscience, Psychology, and Economics, 2,* 12-20. doi: 10. 1037/a0015457.

Logue, A. W. (1988). Research on self-control: An integrating framework. *Behavioral and Brain Sciences, 11*, 665-709. doi: 10. 1017/S0140525X00053978.

Mazur, J. E. (2000). Tradeoffs among delay, rate, and amount of reinforcement. *Behavioural Processes, 49*, 1-10. doi: 10. 1016/S0376-6357(00)00070-X.

Metcalfe, J. , & Mischel, W. (1999). A hot/cool-system analysis of delay of gratification: Dynamics of willpower. *Psychological Review, 106*, 3-19. doi: 10. 1037/0033-295X. 106. 1. 3.

Mischel, W. , Shoda, Y. , & Rodriguez, M. L. (1989). Delay of gratification in children. *Science, 244*, 933-938. doi: 10. 1126/science. 2658056.

Miyata, H. , & Fujita, K. (2008). Pigeons (*Columba livia*) plan future moves on computerized maze tasks. *Animal Cognition, 11,* 505-516. doi: 10. 1007/s10071-008-0141-8.

Murray, E. A. , Kralik, J. D. , Wise, S. P. (2005). Learning to inhibit prepotent responses: Successful performance by rhesus macaques, *Macacamulatta,* on the reversed-contingency task. *Animal Behavior, 69,* 991-998. doi: 10. 1016/j. anbehav. 2004. 06. 034.

Pongracz, P. , Miklosi, A. , Kubinyi, E. , Gurobi, K. , Topal, J. , & Csanyi, V. (2001). Social learning in dogs: the effect of a human demonstrator on the performance of dogs in a detour task. *Animal Behaviour, 62,* 1109–1117. doi: 10. 1006/anbe. 2001. 1866.

Posner, M. I. , & Rothbart, M. K. (1998). Attention, self-regulation, and consciousness. *Philosophical Transactions of the Royal Society of London, 353,* 1915-1927. doi:10. 1098/rstb. 1998. 0344.

Posner, M. I. , & Rothbart, M. K. (2000). Developing mechanisms of self-regulation. *Development and Psychopathology, 12,* 427-441. doi:10. 1017/S0954579400003096.

Poucet, B. , Thinus-Blanc, C. , & Chapuis, N. (1983). Route planning in cats, in relation to the visibility of the goal. *Animal Behaviour, 31,* 594–599. doi:10. 1016/S0003-3472(83)80083-9.

Rachlin, H. (2000). *The science of self-control.* Cambridge, MA: Harvard University Press.

Regolin, L. , Vallortigara, G. , & Zanforlin, M. (1995). Object and spatial representations in detour problems by chicks. *Animal Behaviour 49,* 195–199. doi: 10. 1016/0003-3472(95)80167-7.

Richardson, W. K. , Washburn, D. A. , Hopkins, W. D. , Savage-Rumbaugh, S. E. , & Rumbaugh, D. M. (1990). The NASA/LRC computerized test system. *Behavior Research Methods, Instruments, & Computers, 22,* 127-131.

Santos, L. R. , Ericson, B. N. , Hauser, M. D. (1999). Constraints on problem solving and inhibition: Object retrieval in cotton-top tamarins (*Saguinusoedipusoedipus*). *Journal of Comparative Psychology, 113,* 186-193. doi:10. 1037//0735-7036. 113. 2. 186.

Shamosh, N. A. , DeYoung, C. G. , Green, A. E. , Reis, D. L. , Johnson, M. R. , Conway, A. R. A. , et al. (2008). Individual differences in delay discounting: Relation to intelligence, working memory, and the anterior prefrontal cortex. *Psychological Science, 19*, 904-911. doi: 10. 1111/j. 1467-9280. 2008. 02175. x.

Silberberg, A. , & Fujita, K. (1996). Pointing at smaller food amounts in an analogue of Boysen and Berntson's (1995) procedure. *Journal of the Experimental Analysis of Behavior, 66*, 143-147. doi: 10. 1901/jeab. 1996. 66-143.

Stevens, J. R. , Rosati, A. G. , Ross, K. R. & Hauser, M. D. (2005). Will travel for food: Spatial discounting in two new world monkeys. *Current Biology, 15*, 1855-1860. doi:10. 1016/j. cub. 2005. 09. 016.

Szalda-Petree, A. D. , Craft, B. B. , Martin, L. M. , & Deditius-Island, H. K. (2004). Self-control in rhesus macaques (*Macacamulatta*): Controlling for differential stimulus exposure. *Perceptual and Motor Skills, 98*, 141-146. doi:10. 2466/pms. 98. 1. 141-146.

Tobin, H. , Chelonis, J. J. , & Logue, A. W. (1993). Choice in self-control paradigms using rats. *Psychological Record, 43*, 441-454.

Tobin, H. & Logue, A. W. (1994). Self-control across species (*Columba livia, Homo sapiens*, and *Rattusnorvegicus*). *Journal of Comparative Psychology, 108*, 126-133. doi:10. 1037//0735-7036. 108. 2. 126.

Tobin, H. , Logue, A. W. , Chelonis, J. J. , Ackerman, K. T. , & May, J. G. (1996). Self-control in the monkey *Macacafascicularis*. *Animal Learning and Behavior, 24*, 168-174.

Toner, I. J. , & Smith, R. A. (1977). Age and overt verbalization in delay-maintenance behavior in children. *Journal of Experimental Child Psychology, 24*, 123-128. doi: 10. 1016/0022-0965(77)90025-X.

Vick, S. -J. , Bove, D. & Anderson, J. R. (2010). How do African grey parrots (*Psittacuserithacus*) perform on a delay of gratification task? Animal Cognition, 13, 351-358. doi: 10. 1007/s10071-009-0284-2.

Vlamings, P. H. J. M. , Hare, B. , & Call, J. (2010). Reaching around barriers: the performance of the great apes and 3–5-year-old children. *Animal Cognition*, 13, 273-285. doi: 10. 1007/s10071-009-0265-5.

Vlamings, P. H. J. M. , Uher, J. , & Call, J. (2006). How the great apes (*Pan troglodytes, Pongopygmaeus, Pan paniscus*, and *Gorilla gorilla*) perform on a reversed contingency task:The effects of food quantity and food visibility. *Journal of Experimental Psychology: Animal Behavior Processes, 32*, 60-70. doi: 10. 1037/0097-7403. 32. 1. 60.

Wallis, J. D. , Dias, R. , Robbins, T. W. , & Roberts, A. C. (2001). Dissociable contributions of the orbitofrontal and lateral prefrontal cortex of the marmoset to performance on a detour reaching task. *European Journal of Neuroscience, 13,* 1797-1808. doi: 10. 1046/j. 0953-816x. 2001. 01546. x.

Washburn, D. A. , Hopkins, W. D. , & Rumbaugh, D. M. (1991). Perceived control in rhesus monkeys (*Macacamulatta*): Enhanced video-task performance. *Journal of Experimental Psychology: Animal Behavior Processes, 17*, 123-129. doi: 10. 1037/0097-7403. 17. 2. 123.

Washburn, D. A. , & Rumbaugh, D. M. (1992). Comparative assessment of psychomotor performance: Target prediction by humans and macaques (*Macacamulatta*). *Journal of Experimental Psychology: General, 121*, 305-312. doi: 10. 1037/0097-7403. 17. 2. 123.

Zucca, P. , Antonelli, F. , & Vallortigara, G. (2005). Detour behaviour in three species of birds: Quails (*Coturnix sp.*), herring gulls (*Laruscachinnans*) and canaries (*Serinuscanaria*). *Animal Cognition, 8,* 122-128. doi: 10. 1007/s10071-004-0243-x.

In: Psychology of Self-Control
Editors: A. Durante, et. al.

ISBN: 978-1-61470-881-0
© 2012 Nova Science Publishers, Inc.

Chapter 5

SOCIALISATION AND LOW SELF-CONTROL. A GENDER SPECIFIC ANALYSIS OF IMPULSIVITY AND AGGRESSION

Lieven Pauwels[1]* *and Robert Svensson*[2]†
[1]Ghent University
Department of Criminology and Penal Law
Research group Social Analysis of Security
Universiteitstraat 4, 9000 Gent
Belgium
[2]Faculty of Health and Society
Malmö University
SE- 205 06 Malmö
Sweden

Abstract

Low self-control is an important and stable predictor of offending. Low self-control is often thought of as a multidimensional trait (Gottfredson & Hirschi, 1990). Key dimensions are impulsivity; aggression and risk-taking behaviour. The aim of this paper is to explain

---

* E-mail address: lieven. pauwels@ugent. be
† E-mail address: . svensson@mah. se

individual differences in low self-control as one latent construct and two of its dimensions, namely impulsivity and aggression. It is well established that low levels of self-control increase the risk of offending. However, there is less empirical research that focuses on the role of family structure and socialisation on impulsivity and aggression, two key dimensions of low-self control. Similarly, few research has posed the question to what extent such a model holds for both boys and girls. Therefore the main research question for this study is to explain to what extent family structure, parental attachment, parental control, the school social bond and antisocial values have a direct effect on low self-control (impulsivity and aggression). The data are drawn from a sample of young adolescents in Antwerp, Belgium (N = 2,486). The results show that parental control, parental attachment and the school social bond have direct effects on individual differences in low self-control, regardless of family structure. These effects are by and large mediated by antisocial values. The results are highly equivalent for boys and girls and are hardly different for both dimensions of low self-control: impulsivity and aggression. Implications for further studies are discussed.

Keywords: Low self-control, impulsivity, aggression, socialisation, antisocial values.

INTRODUCTION

It is well known that low levels of self-control increase the risk of offending. One of the most influential criminological theories, at present, is Gottfredson & Hirschi's 1990 General Theory of Crime (or Self-Control Theory). Their theory is based upon the idea that *"human conduct can be understood as the self-interested pursuit of pleasure or the avoidance of pain"* (ibid. p. 5) and that acts of crime are no different from any other acts in this respect. They define crime as *"acts of force or fraud undertaken in the pursuit of self-interest" (ibid. p. 15)*. The theory's fundamental claim is that low self-control is *"the primary individual characteristic causing criminal behavior" (ibid. p. 111)*. Low self-control is seen as a trait, or a summary construct of individual traits including impulsivity, insensitivity, risk-taking and short-sightedness, that have *"a considerable tendency/.../ to come together in the same people, /.../persist through life" (ibid. pp. 90-91)* and which are established very early in life. The theory explains individual differences in crime involvement as variation "in the extent to which [individuals] are vulnerable to the temptations of the moment" (ibid. p. 87). Individuals with low self-control are more vulnerable to temptations of the moment because they fail "to consider the negative or painful consequences of [their] acts and therefore are more likely to engage in acts of crime. Hence, individuals differ in their propensity to engage in crime based on their level of self-control. Gottfredson & Hirschi argue, therefore, that the family environment is the most important and that "the major'cause' of low self-control /.../ appears to be ineffective child-rearing" (ibid p. 97); "self-control differences seem primarily attributed to family socialization practises" (ibid. p. 107). Gottfredson & Hirschi do not insist that other institutions (schools, in particular) cannot play a role but posit that "it is difficult for subsequent institutions to make up for deficiencies" (ibid. p. 107).

The main arguments of their theory thus appear to be that defective early childhood family socialisation (i. e. "the absence of nurturance, discipline, or training" to counteract the natural pursuit of self-interest) causes poor self-control (e. g. , being impulsive, insensitive, risk-taking, etc.) and, in turn, poor self-control causes involvement in crime. Many studies focused on the effects of low levels of self-control on offending, while less research focuses on low self-control and its key dimensions as dependent variables. To gain empirical insight in the causes of low self-control is thus to get insight on the role the socialization variables play in the explanation of low self-control. Therefore the main research question for this study is (1) to examine to what extent family structure, parental attachment, parental control, the school social bond (sometimes called attachment to school) and antisocial values affect the explanation of individual differences in low self-control, as an overall latent construct, (2) to examine to what extent family structure, parental attachment, parental control, the school social bond and antisocial values affect the explanation of individual differences in two key dimensions of low self-control, i. e. impulsivity and aggression and (3) to conduct the aforementioned analyses separate for boys and girls. These questions are not only important from a theoretical point of view, but also from a policy-oriented point of view. The prevention of crime should not be exclusively orientated towards the direct causes of offending, but also towards the causes of the causes of offending. In contemporary theoretical frameworks explaining individual differences in offending, such as the situational action theory (Wikström, 2004), the causes of low self-control are considered to be important indirect causes of offending.

THE THEORY OF LOW SELF-CONTROL IN A NUTSHELL

The question why some people restrain from committing acts of crime is not only a question raised by criminologists. Many sociologists consider the same question from another point of view: they regard the process of socializing as a continuing key issue in sociology. As originally conceptualized by Gottfredson and Hirschi (1990: 232), low self-control is argued to be *"the individual-level cause of crime"*, i. e. low self-control is theorised to be the primary explanation for criminal behaviour. The effects of all other theoretical constructs to explain offending are spurious when self-control is entered into the equation. While several scholars have issued critiques of the theory (Akers, 1991; Barlow, 1991; Benson & Moore, 1992; Cohen & Vila, 1996; Geis, 2000; Reed & Yeager, 1996; Tittle, 1991), it also attained considerable empirical support. Low self-control has consistently been found to be a modest to strong correlate of both crime and analogous acts of deviant behaviour, including substance use and or abuse. [*] Ineffective child-rearing (inconsequente parenting) seems to be the major cause of low self-control according to the authors. Self-control is established early in life as a consequence of the socialization process. Gottfredson & Hirschi stress the importance of parental supervision, monitoring, discipline and affection.

CAUSES OF LOW SELF-CONTROL

In a previous study on the importance of family processes in the development of self-control. Hope, Grasmick, & Pointon (2003) and Vazsonyi & Belliston (2007) noted that only few studies have examined the causes of low self-control consistent with self-control theory (see also Pratt et al. , 2004). In other words, many studies to date have focused on the self-control–offending relationship and have not included aspects of the family structure and social bonds in empirical tests of the theory. This is so despite the fact that Gottfredson and Hirschi clearly point to the importance of the family as the

---

[*] For a good overview see: Arneklev et al. , 1993; Cochran, Wood et al. , 1994; Evans et al. , 1997; Gibbs and Giever, 1995; Paternoster and Brame, 1998; Pratt and Cullen, 2000; Brownfield and Sorensen, 1993; Gibbs et al, 2003; Grasmick et al. 1993; Piquero and Rosay, 1998; Piquero and Tibbetts, 1996; Ribeaud and Eisner 2006; Sorenson and Brownfield, 1995; Turner and Piquero 2002; Vazsonyi et al. 2001; Wood et al. , , 1993.

primary socializing agent responsible for the development of self-control. The family is the primary unit in which children learn values and attitudes that guide them throughout their lives. In a cross-cultural and cros-national test of self-control theory Vazsonyi & Belliston (2007) were able to demonstrate the relationships between the family processes of monitoring, closeness and support, self-control and offending. Vazsonyi & Belliston (2007) demonstrated both direct and indirect effects of socialization variables on offending. Self-control was a key mediator of the relationship between family social processes and offending, while still direct effects of family mechanisms on offending were found. Families do not only differ in levels of child rearing, but also differ in their family structure. Some children grow up in one-parent families while others grow up in families with two caretakers. Growing up in a one-parent family may be an indicator of experienced family disruption and may therefore have a lasting impact on the ways these children grow up and develop self-control. Parents act as agents of informal control and when a breakdown in the family structure occurs, it may be a consequence that these children get involved in antisocial behaviour. Adolescents who have experienced a family break-up may be more likely to demonstrate antisocial behavior (Siegel & Welsh, 2009). This study therefore tests the assumption that family structure (i. e. growing up in a one-parent family) is indirectly related to low-self control, through the mediating role of mechanisms of social bonding, such as attachment to parents, the school social bond and antisocial values. We test the hypotheses that these mechanisms play an important role in the socialization process of the child and thus in the development of low self-control. It has been stated that *"when socialization is effective, norms will be internalized and, as a consequence, an individual's conscience, or superego, will be well developed. If the level of attachment to parents is poor, however, it is hypothesized that the internalization of norms and the development of conscience will be adversely affected" (Svensson, 2004:479).*

Low self-control is thus conceptualized as a consequence of one's family structure, attachment to parents, the school social bond and one's level of antisocial values. There is a great number of empirical studies that have found support that low levels of morality are related to offending (e. g. Agnew, 2003; Chapple et al. , 2005; Costello & Vowell, 1999; Hirschi, 1969; Pauwels, 2007; Svensson, 2004; Svensson & Pauwels, 2010; Wikström & Butterworth, 2006). Earlier, Deklerck & Pauwels (2010) demonstrated that low levels of morality (or high levels of antisocial values) was a strong predictor for both low self-control and offending in two independently drawn urban samples in Belgium.

Therefore we include antisocial values as a predictor of low self-control in the present study.

In the present study, family structure is considered to be the "structural background of low self-control". Social bonds are considered to be "causes of the causes" of low self-control, i. e. they play a major role in explaining low self-control for adolescent boys and girls, while moral values is considered to be the key mediator of the relation between the aforementioned variables and low self-control.

HOW INVARIANT ARE THE CAUSES OF LOW SELF-CONTROL BY GENDER?

It is well established that males commit more offences and more serious offences than females in bivariate and multivariate studies of both self-reported and officially recorded delinquency (e. g. Junger-Tas et al. , 1994). One important task facing criminology is that of developing theoretical frameworks in which differences may be understood and explained. Most traditional theories focus explicitly on male delinquency (Bartush & Matsueda, 1996) and several researchers have concluded that more research is needed to test the gender gap in these theories (e. g. , Bruinsma & Lissenberg, 1987; Liu & Kaplan, 1999; Svensson, 2004). When the gender gap in the aetiology of offending has been discussed, it is often assumed that differences in the socialization of males and females within the family are responsible for gender differences (e. g. Moffitt et al. , 2001; Giordano & Cernkovich, 1997; Lanctôt & LeBlanc, 2002). Other researchers focused on differences in self-control (Burton et al. , 1998; Blackwell & Piquero, 2004) and morality (Wikström & Butterworth, 2006; Svensson, 2004) to account for gender differences. It is not uncommon in criminological inquiries for attributes like sex and race to be included as predictors. In the case of sex some researchers even (wrongly) claim that it is the best predictor of criminal involvement. The problem with the common practice of including attributes as predictors is that they may confuse our search for causes and explanation of crime, and even more worryingly, they may make people think that the fact, for example, that someone is male or black could be a cause of their level of self-control.

We argue that it is important to distinguish between causes and correlates and instead focus on the general nature of an assumption of how causal processes affect low self-control. We argue that statistical prediction through regression models does not equal causation, and that for a factor to qualify as a cause we need to make a case that it has some kind of powers to initiate a causal process that produces the effect. It is difficult to see, for example, how being male could constitute a cause of low self-control (i. e. , be a factor that initiates a causal process resulting in an act of crime).

This does not mean that characteristics that are relevant in the causation of low self-control might not be more prevalent, for example, amongst males but the point is that it is these characteristics that we should focus on as causal factors in our explanations rather than the fact that the person is male. In principle, if we can measure the real causative factors (in the present case: social bonds and antisocial values) there is no need to include attributes like gender (biological sex of the respondents) that at best are 'markers' of the real causative factors among the predictors in our studies.

The main point is that while the correlation between attributes and low self-control can be explained, attributes cannot explain why some people have low levels of self-control. This very important insight has significant implications for what research questions can be posed concerning the causes of low self-control and what conclusions for crime prevention can be drawn from research findings about correlations between attributes and low self-control. The fact that a person's sex to some degree may predict his or her low self-control does not mean that his or her sex causes his or her level of self-control. At best it can be a marker of causes associated with a particular attribute. We are convinced of the fact that we should avoid including attributes as (potential) causes in causal models which aim to explain what causes people's level of low self-control. [*] On the other hand it is challenging to find about how similar or different causal mechanisms operate by gender.

THE PRESENT STUDY

This study thus aims at testing the independent effects of family background, socialisation variables on low self-control as a general construct and two of its key dimensions, impulsivity and aggression. At the same time, this study aims at detecting similarities and differences between boys and girls in the explanation of low self-control and the impact of socialisation variables.

---

[*] We might include gender if the goal is solely to predict people's risk of having low self-control, but that would be in our view an analysis that lacks a theoretical rationale.

We explicitly assume that one's family background only explain differences in low self-control as far as the socialisation process is not included in the equations. One-parent families might face more difficulties in socializing adolescents because only one parent (or caretaker) is socializing the child. If that hypothesis is correct, then no effect can be found of family structure when control is held of social bonds. Social bonding variables includes measures such as parental attachment, the school social bond, parental control. We assume that antisocial values is the key mediator of parental attachment, the school social bond, parental control in the explanation of low self-control. We test the assumption of equality of effects by rerunning the analyses separately for boys and girls. Finally we run all models for two key dimensions of low self-control, impulsivity and aggression.

DATA

The Antwerp school survey

Antwerp, one of the largest cities in Belgium has a population of approximately 500,000 inhabitants (including suburbs). The Antwerp school survey included all first grade students (in the Belgian school system) that both lived in the city of Antwerp *and* went to school in Antwerp. [*] The survey thus constitutes of 2,486 first-graders attending 23 secondary schools in Antwerp. The average age of this population is thirteen years at the time they enter the first grade and fourteen years when they leave the first grade. The study was conducted between January and June of 2005. Scholars distributed the questionnaires and the students completed the questionnaires during lesson time in the presence of the researcher. The non-response rate for the Antwerp sample was 7. 5%. The Antwerp sample consisted of 49. 4% boys and 50. 6% girls. Almost half of the respondents had a fully native background (both parents of Belgian descent), ten percent of the respondents had one parent with an immigrant background, while 45. 5% of the respondents had two parents with an immigrant background. Obviously, there is an overrepresentation of students with an immigrant background, which is due to a higher level of participation among schools in inner city areas. Almost three quarters of the respondents were aged 12-14, while 26. 2% of the respondents were aged 15-

---

[*] These students are approximately aged 12 to 14.

17. 15% of the respondents lived in a single parent or one caregiver family and 85% of the respondents lived with two parents or caregivers.

MEASUREMENT OF CONSTRUCTS AND DESCRIPTIVES

Low self-control is an additive index primarily based on the items used and developed by Grasmick et al. (1993). The construct measures whether an individual lacks the ability to resist temptations and provocations. The overall scale is based on seven items with a scale Alpha of . 78 High values on the measure indicate a low level of self-control. The general low self-control scale is two-dimensional and contains an impulsivity scale (four items: alpha: 0. 708) and an aggression scale based on tree items (Alpha: 0. 572). Factor analysis revealed that both dimensions are strongly correlated (r = 0. 59***). Detailed information on the wording of the items is provided in Appendix I.

Mechanisms of socialisation

Table 1. Descriptives of variables in the analysis

	Range	*Mean*	*SD*
Family structure	0-1	. 15	-
Antisocial values	4-20	9. 91	4. 36
Low self-control	7-35	21. 19	6. 33
Parental control	5-25	19. 58	4. 38
School social bond	5-25	18. 27	3. 91
Parental attachment	4-20	17. 06	3. 25
Aggression	3-15	8. 60	3. 24
Impulsivity	4-20	12. 59	3. 96

We distinguish between mechanisms of social bonding and antisocial values. Social bonds include parental attachment, parental control (monitoring) and the school social bond (sometimes referred to as attachment to school).

Parental attachment is an additive index and measured by four items (Alpha: . 81). The school social bond is also an additive index and measured by three items and the Alpha level is . 65. Finally, parental control (monitoring) is measured by five items in Antwerp with an Alpha level of . 71. The antisocial values scale is adapted from the Sampson & Bartush (1998) legal cynicism scale and is based on four items. The antisocial values scale take the form of an additive index with scale Alpha of . 78. High values on this scale indicate a high level of antisocial values.

Family structure is coded as zero if the respondent is living with two parents and one if the respondent is living in a single parent family. For a description of all of the variables included in the analysis, see Table 1.

STRATEGY OF ANALYSIS AND FINDINGS

The analyses were carried out by using a series of block wise OLS regression models. Three block wise regression models were estimated for low self-control, impulsivity and aggression, respectively. In the first model only family structure is included. In the second model, parental control, the school social bond and parental attachment were added to get estimations of the independent effects of informal controls above and beyond family structure. Finally antisocial values is added into the equation as this concept is thought of as a key mechanism in understanding individual differences in low self-control. All analyses are conducted separately for boys and girls and for both dimensions of low self-control.

Predicting low self-control by gender

In Table 2 low self-control is regressed on the independent variables. In the first model the results show that single parent family is related with low self-control for girls, but not for boys. The effect of single parent family is, however, rather weak. The squared multiple correlation is very low, indicating that no adequate predictions can be made when using family structure as a predictor of low self-control. The effect of single parent on self-control is still significant in model 2 when control is held for the school social bond, parental attachment and parental control. For boys, only the school bond and parental control are significantly and negatively related with low self-control. The inclusion of social bonding variables increases the squared multiple correlation (0. 16 for boys and 0. 23 for girls. In model 2 the school social bond, parental attachment and parental control are significantly and negatively related with low self-control for girls. The school social bond seems to have the strongest independent effect for both boys and girls. The effects of social bonding variables decrease when control is held for antisocial values in model 3. For boys, the effect of parental control is fully mediated by antisocial values. For girls this is not entirely true, although the effect has strongly decreased. Antisocial values has the strongest positive effect on low self-control for both boys and girls. Interestingly, the squared multiple correlation explains 34% of the variance in low self-control for boys and 38% of the variance for girls. The model fit is somewhat better for girls than for boys. The pattern is, however, highly similar. In the next step we asses to what extent differences or similarities can be detected for the two key dimensions of low self-control, namely impulsivity and aggression.

Table 2. OLS regression analysis predicting low self control by gender

Dependent: Low self-control	Model 1 Boys	Model 1 Girls	Model 2 Boys	Model 2 Girls	Model 3 Boys	Model 3 Girls
	Beta	Beta	Beta	Beta	Beta	Beta
Structural background						
Single parent family	. 02	. 10**	-. 01	. 07**	-. 01	. 07**
Socialization variables						
School social bond			-. 29***	-. 30***	-. 17***	-. 15***
Parental attachment			-. 03	-. 08**	. 01	-. 06*
Parental control			-. 18***	-. 21***	-. 03	-. 08**
Antisocial Values					-49***	-. 46***
R^2	. 00	. 01	. 16	. 23	. 34	. 38

$* p < . 05; ** p < . 01; *** p < . 001.$

Predicting impulsivity by gender

Table 3 presents the findings predicting impulsivity for boys and girls. The results show that single parent family has a weak and positive direct effect on impulsivity for girls but not for boys. The squared multiple correlation is zero for boys and 1% for girls. Knowledge on family structure is not successful in predicting impulsivity. In model 2 both the school social bond and parental control have independent negative effects on impulsivity for both boys and girls, while parental attachment does not seem to matter. The effect of the school social bond is still significant when control is held for antisocial values for boys and girls. The relationship between parental control and impulsivity is not significant in this model for boys. The relationship between parental control and impulsivity is thus fully mediated by antisocial values for boys, but not for girls. For girls, parental control has still an independent effect on impulsivity, although the effect has decreased. Antisocial values has the largest independent direct effect on explaining impulsivity for both boys and girls.

Table 3. OLS regression analysis predicting impulsivity by gender

Dependent: Impulsivity	Model 1 Boys	Model 1 Girls	Model 2 Boys	Model 2 Girls	Model 3 Boys	Model 3 Girls
	Beta	Beta	Beta	Beta	Beta	Beta
Structural background						
Single parent family	.02	.10***	-.01	.08**	-.01	.08**
Socialization variables						
School social bond			-.33***	-.33***	-.22***	-.20***
Parental attachment			-.05	-.05	-.02	-.03
Parental control			-.14***	-.23***	-.01	-.11***
Antisocial Values					.43***	.40***
R^2	.00	.01	.18	.24	.32	.36

* $p < .05$; ** $p < .01$; *** $p < .001$.

Predicting aggression by gender

The results in table 4 indicate that single parent family has a weak and positive direct effect on aggression for girls but not for boys. The squared multiple correlation is zero for boys and zero for girls. Knowledge on family structure is not successful in predicting aggression. The results in Table 4 further indicate that the school social bond and parental control are both significantly and negatively related to aggression for both boys and girls. Parental attachment has also a negative effect on aggression for girls, but not for boys. In the third model, when antisocial values is also included, the effect school social bond and parental control on aggression r vanishes totally for boys and seriously decreases for girls. Parental attachment is, however, still directly and negatively related to aggression when control is held for antisocial values for girls. As for impulsivity, antisocial values has the strongest direct independent effect on aggression. This pattern is the same for both boys and girls.

Table 4. OLS regression analysis predicting aggression by gender

Dependent: Aggression	Model 1 Boys	Model 1 Girls	Model 2 Boys	Model 2 Girls	Model 3 Boys	Model 3 Girls
	Beta	Beta	Beta	Beta	Beta	Beta
Structural background						
Single parent family	. 01	. 06*	-. 00	. 04	-. 00	. 04
Informal controls						
School social bond			-. 17***	-. 18***	-. 06*	-. 05
Parental attachment			-. 00	-. 10**	. 03	-. 08**
Parental control			-. 18***	-. 12***	-. 05	-. 02
Antisocial Values					. 42***	. 40***
R^2	. 00	. 00	. 08	. 11	. 21	. 22
Adj. R^2	-. 00	. 00	. 08	. 10	. 21	. 22

* $p < . 05$; ** $p < . 01$; *** $p < . 001$.

CONCLUSION AND DISCUSSION

This study found that family structure hardly affects low self-control among a sample of Belgian boys and girls. There was a rather small bivariate effects found for girls, but that effect diminished as soon as social bonds and antisocial values were taken into account. The effect of family structure on low self-control remains therefore ambiguous. The results indicate that the school social bond and parental control are the most important mechanism of social bonding in the explanation of low self-control. The effects of these social bonds seriously decrease when antisocial values are entered into the equations. This pattern is found for both boys and girls and has been shown for both aspects of low self-control. The development of antisocial values seems to be a key mechanism in the explanation of low self-control. However, antisocial values cannot be the only mechanism. We argue that a mechanism-based approach to the study of low self-control is of importance to further gain insight in unraveling black boxes. The basic philosophy behind a mechanism-based explanation is that a social phenomenon is explained from precisely those mechanisms that bring about differences and changes in the dependent variable. The Norwegian sociologist Jon Elster (1989: 3-4) has argued that the explanation of an event or act deals with plausible reasons why the event or the act took place. The attention to mechanisms is absolutely nothing new to our proposed style of theorizing and is rooted in the ideas and theories of very influential sociologists such as Robert K. Merton and Emile Durkheim. This way of theorizing is a scientific realist approach of low self-control that is rooted within the tradition of analytical sociology (for a discussion see Hedström & Swedberg, 1998; Hedström, 2005). *"Analytical sociology seeks to explain complex social processes by carefully dissecting them and then bringing into focus their most important constituent components. It is through dissection and analytical abstraction that the important cogs and wheels of social processes are made visible and intelligible" (Edling & Hedström, 2005:1).* An analytical approach to low self-control differs from classic criminological studies of the causes and consequences of low self-control in that much more attempts are undertaken to visualize and expose the social processes that are actually at work when an explanation of low self-control is formulated.

APPENDIX 1. MEASURES EMPLOYED IN THE STUDY

<u>Low self-control</u>

Impulsivity
I often do things without thinking first
/ I have fun when I can, even if I get into trouble afterwards / I say what I think, even if it's not smart / I often do what I want to /

Aggression
when angry, others would better stay away from me/ when I am angry, I'd rather hit than talk/ I am able to quietly discuss quarrels (R)

Five point scale: totally agree / agree / neither agree nor disagree / disagree / totally disagree

<u>Morality (Antisocial values)</u>

Rules are made to be broken / ok to break rules, as long as do not get caught / fighting ok when provoked / if honest ways to achieve something fail, then use dishonest ways

Five point scale: totally agree/ agree/ neither agree nor disagree/ disagree/ totally disagree

<u>*Parental control:*</u>

Parents know whom I hang around with / parents know where I am when not at home / parents know how I behave when not at home

Five point scale: totally agree/ agree/ nor agree nor disagree/ disagree/ totally disagree

<u>*Parental attachment:*</u>

Getting along with parents/ remarks of parents are important/ likes to spend free time with parents/ talk with parents if I have a problem

Five point scale: totally agree/ agree/ nor agree nor disagree/ disagree/ totally disagree

---

School social bond:

Studying is important to me/ no efforts home work/ not interested in high grades/ always studying/ don't care what teachers say

Five point scale: totally agree/ agree/ nor agree nor disagree/ disagree/ totally disagree

---

The results of the present study are valuable, not only from a theoretical point of view, but also when considering the prevention of offending. Without a thorough knowledge on crime causation, prevention seems a rather difficult or even impossible task.

Prevention should be guided towards the main causes of offending, but in addition to the" causes of the causes" of offending. Our study confirms that social bonds are strongly related to low self-control, especially through the effect of antisocial values. These results are highly similar for boys and girls. Based on these findings we argue that it is important to focus on parent-child relations and commitment to school to diminish one's antisocial values and to increase one's level of self-control.

However, the present study has some important limitations that should be taken into account. First of all, the study is cross-sectional and examined the strength of the statistical association between a series of independent variables and low self-control. Therefore we must be careful with causal interpretations. Second, the empirical model has causal arrows in one direction and does not take feedback loops into account. It is possible that low self-control in itself further affects antisocial values, but such a design would require instrumental variables to test feedback loops and such measures were not available in the present study.

Unfortunately, as this study was merely from a theoretically point of view focusing on the role of social bonding variables as key mechanisms in the explanation of low self-control (as measured as an overall index of impulsivity and aggression and re-analyzed for both dimensions), it is impossible to derive from this study how effective crime prevention policy which focuses on the strengthening of social bonds, moral values and self-control should be organised. It takes evaluation studies to answer the latter research problem, but it takes hypothesis testing as a guideline. Therefore hypothesis testing and criminal policy are inevitably intertwined.

REFERENCES

Agnew, R. (2003). The interactive effects of social control variables on delinquency. In C. L. Britt and M. R. Gottfredson (Eds), *Control theories of crime and delinquency. Advances in criminological theory, vol. 12.*, New Brunswick: Transaction Publishers.

Akers, R. (1991). Self-Control as a general theory of crime. *Journal of Quantitative Criminology* 7:201-211.

Arneklev, B. , Grasmick, H. , Tittle, C. & Bursik, R. (1993). Low self-control and imprudent behavior. *Journal of Quantitative Criminology* 9:225-247.

Barlow, H. (1991). Explaining crime and analogous acts, or the unrestrained will grab at pleasure wherever they can. *Journal of Criminal Law and Criminology* 82:229-242.

Bartush, D. J. , & Matsueda, R. L. (1996). Gender, Reflected Appraisals, and Labelling: A cross group test of an interactionist theory of delinquency. *Social Forces,* 75, 145-176.

Benson, M. L. & Moore, E. (1992). Are white-collar and common offenders the same? *Journal of Research in Crime and Delinquency* 29:251-272.

Blackwell, B. S. , & Piquero, A. R. (2004). On the relationships between gender, power control, self-control, and crime. Journal of Criminal Justice, 33, 1-17.

Bruinsma, G. , & Lissenberg, E. (1987) Vrouwen als Daders. In G. Bruinsma (Ed.), Vrouw en Criminaliteit, Vrouwen als Plegers en Slachtoffers van Criminaliteit. Amsterdam: Boom Appel.

Brownfield, D. & Sorenson, A. M. . (1999). Self control and juvenile delinquency: theoretical issues and an empirical assessment of selected elements of a general theory of crime. *Deviant Behavior* 14:243-264.

Burton, V. S. Jr, Cullen, F. T. , Evans, T. D. , Alarid, Leanne F. , & Dunaway R. G. (1998). Gender, Self-Control, and Crime. Journal of Research in Crime and Delinquency, 35, 123-147.

Chapple, C. , McQuillan, J. & Berdahl, T. (2005). Gender, social bonds, and delinquency: a comparison of boys' and girls' models. *Social Science Research* 34: 357-383.

Cochran, J. , Wood, P. & Arneklev, B. (1994). Is the Religiosity-Delinquency Relationship Spurious? A test of arousal and social control theories. *Journal of Research in Crime and Delinquency* 31:92-123.

Cohen, L. & Vila, B. (1996). Self- control and social control: an exposition of the Gottfredson-Hirschi/Sampson-Laub debate. Studies in Crime and Crime Prevention 5:125-150.

Costello, B. & Vowell, P. (1999). Testing control theory and differential

association: a reanalysis of the Richmond youth project data. Criminology 37:815-842.

Deklerck, N. & Pauwels; L. (2010). *Individu, omgeving en de verklaring van jeugdcrimineel gedrag, een toets in twee stedelijke settings*. Antwerpen: Maklu

Edling, C. , Hedström, P. (2005). *Analytical Sociology In Tocqueville'S Democracy In America*. Working Paper No. 3. Department Of Sociology. Stockholm University.

Elster, J. 1989. *Nuts And Bolts For The Social Sciences*. Cambridge: Cambridge University Press.

Evans, T. , Cullen, F. , Burton, V. , Dunaway, R. & Benson, M. (1997). The social consequences of self-control: testing the general theory of crime. *Criminology* 35:475- 501.

Geis, G. (2000). On the absence of self-control as the basis for a general theory of crime: a critique. *Theoretical Criminology* 4:35-53.

Gibbs,J & Giever, D. (1995). Self-control and its manifestations among university students: an empirical test of Gottfredson and Hirschi's general theory. *Justice Quarterly* 12:231-255.

Gibbs, J. , Giever, D. & Higgins, G. (2003). A test of Gottfredson and Hirschi's general theory using structural equation modeling. *Criminal Justice and Behavior* 30:441-458.

Giordano, P. C. , & Cernkovich, S. A. (1997). Gender and Antisocial Behavior. In D. M. Stoff, J. Breiling and J. D. Maser (Eds.), Handbook of Antisocial Behavior (496-510). New York: Wiley.

Gottfredson, M. R. & Hirschi, T. (1990). *A general theory of crime*. Stanford, CA: Stanford University Press.

Grasmick, H. , Tittle, C. , Bursik, R. & Arneklev, B. (1993). Testing the core empirical implications of Gottfredson and Hirschi's general theory of crime. *Journal of Research in Crime and Delinquency* 30:5-29.

Hedström, P. , 2005. *Dissecting The Social. On The Principles Of Analytical Sociology*. Cambridge: Cambridge University Press.

Hedström, P. , Swedberg, R. , (Eds.). 1998. *Social Mechanisms: An Analytical Approach To Social Theory*. Cambridge: Cambridge University Press.

Hirschi, T. (1969). *Causes of delinquency*. Berkeley: University of California Press.

Hope, T. L. , Grasmick, H. G. & Pointon, L. J. (2003). The family in Gottfredson and Hirschi's general theory of crime: Structure, parenting and self-control. *Sociological Focus*, 36, 291-311.

Lanctôt, N. , & LeBlanc, M. (2002). *Explaining deviance by adolescent females. In M. Tonry (Ed.), Crime and Justice, vol. 29*. Chicago: University of Chicago Press.

Liu, X. , & Kaplan, H. B. (1999). Explaining the Gender Differences in Adolescent Delinquent Behavior: A Longitudinal Test of Mediating Mechanisms. Criminology, 37, 195-215.

Moffitt, T. E. , Caspi, A. , Rutter, M. , & Silva, P. A. (2001). Sex Differences in Antisocial Behaviour. Cambridge: Cambridge University Press.

Paternoster, R. & Brame, R. (1998). The structural similarity of processes generating criminal and analogous behaviors. Criminology 36:633-670.

Pauwels, L. (2007). Buurtinvloeden en jeugdcriminaliteit. Een toets van de Sociale Desorganisatietheorie. The Hague: Boom Juridische Uitgevers.

Piquero, A. & Rosay, A. (1998). The reliability and validity of Grasmick et al.'s self- control scale: a comment on Longshore et al. Criminology 36: 157-173.

Piquero, A. & Tibbetts, S. (1996). Specifying the direct and indirect effects of low self-control and situational factors in offenders' decision making: toward a more complete model of rational offending. Justice Quarterly 13: 481-510.

Pratt, T. & Cullen, F. (2000). The empirical status of Gottfredson and Hirschi's general theory of crime: a meta-analysis. Criminology 38: 931-964

Reed, G. & Yeager, P. (1996). Organizational offending and neoclassical criminology: challenging the reach of a general theory of crime. Criminology 34: 357-382.

Reiss, A. (1951). Delinquency as a failure of personal and social control. American Sociological Review 16: 196–207.

Ribeaud, D. & Eisner, M. (2006). The'drug-crime link' from a self-control perspective: an empirical test in a Swiss youth sample. European Journal of Criminology 3: 33-67.

Sampson, R. J. & Bartush, D. J. (1998). Legal cynicism and (subcultural?) tolerance of deviance: the neighborhood context of racial differences. Law and Society Review 32: 777-804.

Siegel, L. J. & Welch, B. C. (2009). Juvenile Delinquency: Theory, Practice, and Law, 10th Edition, Wadsworth Publishing Co Inc.

Sorenson, A. M. & Brownfield, D. (1995). Adolescent drug use and a general theory of crime: an analysis of a theoretical integration. Canadian Journal of Criminology 37:19-37.

Svensson, R. (2004). Shame as a consequence of the parent-child relationship: a study of gender differences in juvenile delinquency. *European Journal of Criminology* 1:477-504.

Svensson, R. & Pauwels, L. (2010). Is a risky lifestyle always "risky"? The interaction between individual propensity and lifestyle risk in adolescent offending: A test in two urban samples. *Crime and Delinquency*, 56:608-626.

Tittle, C. (1991). A general theory of crime: a book review. *American Journal of Sociology* 96:1609-1611.

Turner, M. and Piquero, A. (2002). The stability of self-control. *Journal of Criminal Justice* 30:457-471.

Vazsonyi, A. , Pickering, L. , Junger, M. , & Hessing, D. (2001). An empirical test of a general theory of crime: A four nation comparative study of self-control and prediction of deviance. *Journal of Research in Crime and Delinquency* 38: 91-131.

Vazsonyi, A. , Belliston, L. (2007). The family -> low self-control -> deviance. A Cross-Cultural and Cross-National Test of Self-Control Theory. *Criminal Justice and Behavior,* 34 (4) 505-530.

Wikström, P. -O. (2004). Crime as alternative: towards a cross-level situational action theory of crime causation. In: J. McCord (Ed), *Beyond empiricism: Institutions and intentions in the study of crime. Advances in criminological theory,* Volume 13, 1-37. New Brunswick: Transaction.

Wikström, P-O H. (2005). The social origins of pathways in crime. Towards a developmental ecological action theory of crime involvement and its changes. In: D. Farrington (Ed), *Integrated developmental and life-course theories of offending. Advances in Criminological Theory, Volume 14,* 211-246. New Brunswick: Transaction.

Wikström, P-O H. (2006). Individuals, settings and acts of crime. Situational mechanisms and the explanation of crime. In: P-O Wikström and R. Sampson (Eds.), *The explanation of crime: context, mechanisms and development,* 61-107. Cambridge. Cambridge University Press.

Wikström, P. -O. (2007). In search of causes and explanations of crime. In: R. King and E. Wincup (Eds.), *Doing research on crime and justice,* 2nd Edition, 117-140. Oxford: Oxford University Press.

Wikström P. -O. & Butterworth, D. (2006). *Adolescent crime: individual differences and lifestyles.* Collumpton: Willan Publishing.

Wikström, P. -O. & Sampson, R. (2003). Social mechanisms of community influences on crime and pathways in criminality. In: B. Lahey, T. Moffitt and A. Caspi (Eds.), *The causes of conduct disorder and serious juvenile delinquency,* 118-148. New York: Guildford Press.

Wikström, P. -O. & Treiber, K. (2007). The role of self-control in crime causation: Beyond Gottfredson and Hirschi's general theory of crime. *European Journal of Criminology,* 4 (2): 237-264.

Thomas, W. & Bernat, F. (1998). Social learning, self-control, and substance abuse by eighth-grade students: a tale of two cities. *Journal of Drug Issues* 28:539-558.

Wood, P. B. , Pfefferbaum, B. & Arneklev, B. J. (1993). Risk-taking and self-control: social Psychological Correlates of Delinquency. *Journal of Crime and Justice* 16:111-130.

In: Psychology of Self-Control
Editors: A. Durante, et. al.

ISBN: 978-1-61470-881-0
© 2012 Nova Science Publishers, Inc.

Chapter 6

THE 'WHAT' OF DOING: INTROSPECTION-BASED EVIDENCE FOR JAMES'S IDEOMOTOR PRINCIPLE

Christopher C. Berger[1], *John A. Bargh*[2] *and Ezequiel Morsella*[1,3*]

[1]Department of Psychology
San Francisco State University (SFSU)
1600 Holloway Avenue, EP 301
San Francisco, California, U. S.
[2] Department of Psychology
Yale University, Connecticut, U. S.
[3] Department of Neurology
University of California, San Francisco, U. S.

Abstract

Science has begun to illuminate the mechanisms underlying self-control and its phenomenology. One prevalent hypothesis regarding self-directed,'voluntary' action is that of *ideomotor processing* – that both the guidance and knowledge of one's voluntary actions are limited to perceptual-like representations of action outcomes (e. g. , the'image' of

* Email address: morsella@sfsu. edu

one's finger flexing), with the motor programs/events actually responsible for enacting actions being unconscious. To further examine this basic notion empirically, participants performed simple actions (e. g. , sniffing) while introspecting the degree to which they perceived certain body regions to be responsible for the actions. Consistent with ideomotor theory, participants perceived regions (e. g. , the nose) associated with the perceptual consequences of actions (e. g. , sniffing) to be more responsible for the actions than regions (e. g. , chest/torso) actually generating the action. We then examined participants' lay intuitions about perceptual consequences. In addition to supporting ideomotor theory, these findings unveil lay intuitions about the nature of action, perception, and self-control.

> In perfectly simple voluntary acts there is nothing else in the mind but the kinesthetic idea…of what the act is to be.
>
> – James (1890, p. 771).

INTRODUCTION

The television program *60 Minutes* recently presented a news story about how patients can today control robotic arm/limb prostheses. In the episode, the interviewer was surprised to learn that a soldier who had lost his lower arm in combat could, in just a few trials, control the grasping motions of a robotic hand, a prosthesis that was connected to electrodes attached to the muscles of the remaining part of the soldier's upper arm. The interviewer asked the soldier how he knew which muscles to activate in order to enact the action. The soldier replied that he had no idea regarding which muscles to activate, nor what the muscles were actually doing; rather, he claimed that, to enact the action on the part of the robotic arm, all he had to do was imagine the grasping action. This image (or *Effektbild*; Harleß 1861) was somehow translated (unconsciously) into the kind of muscular activation that would normally result in the grasping action. Is this how people generally guide and perceive their own actions?

According to James's (1890) popularization of *ideomotor processing*, the answer is yes. Originating in the times of Lotze (1852), Harleß (1861), and Carpenter (1874), the hypothesis states that action guidance, and action knowledge, are limited to perceptual-like representations (or, *event codes*; cf. , Hommel, Müsseler, Aschersleben, & Prinz 2001) of action outcomes (e. g. , the'image' of one's finger flexing), with the motor programs/events actually responsible for enacting the actions being unconscious (Gray 1995; Gray 2004; Jeannerod 2006; Rosenbaum 2002; Rossetti 2001). (See neuroimaging evidence for the ideomotor principle in Melcher, Weidema, Eenshuistra, Hommel, & Gruber 2008). From this standpoint, conscious contents regarding an ongoing action are primarily of the perceptual consequences of that action (Jeannerod 2006). (For a computational explanation of why motor programs must be unconscious, and explicit memories should be not formed for them, see Grossberg 1999.) Thus, one is unconscious of the complicated programs that calculate which muscles should be activated at a given time, but is often aware of their proprioceptive and perceptual consequences (e. g. , perceiving a finger flex). Consistent with contemporary ideomotor-like approaches (e. g. , Greenwald 1970; Hommel 2009; Hommel & Elsner 2009; Hommel, Müsseler, Aschersleben, & Prinz 2001), James (1890) proposed that the conscious mind later uses these conscious perceptual-like representations to voluntarily guide the generation of motor efference, which itself is an unconscious process.

In today's renaissance of action research (Agnew, Carlston, Graziano, & Kelly, 2009; Hommel et al. 2001; Morsella 2009; Nattkemper & Ziessler 2004), ideomotor processing is one prevalent hypothesis regarding how cognition influences action (Hommel et al. 2001). Although widely accepted, what one can (and cannot) introspect about according to ideomotor theory has never been examined directly. Previous research (e. g. , research on'imageless thought'; Ach 1905/1951; Woodworth 1939) has examined the conscious contents preceding voluntary action, but little if any research had as its focus what one can introspect about while performing an action. Thus, this fundamental aspect of human nature, in which one is conscious of action outcomes but not of action *means*, has never been explored in the psychology laboratory.

Interestingly, not everyone agrees with this overarching hypothesis (see list of four'dissenters' in James, 1890, p. 772). For instance, in a lively debate, one of us (EM) was recently challenged by an expert on biofeedback who claimed that James (1890) and the ideomotor theorists after him got it wrong: The actor *is* aware of the efference to the muscles (Wundt's *feeling of innervation*; cf. , James 1890, p. 771) that are responsible for action outcomes (see review in Scheerer 1987). (Wundt later abandoned the feeling of innervation hypothesis; Klein 1970.) In contrast, James (1890) staunchly proclaimed, "There is no introspective evidence of the feeling of innervation"

(p. 775). Our point is that, though most researchers in the field may agree with James's stance, there needs to be straightforward and citable empirical evidence for this important tenet of ideomotor theory. Thus, we believe that the time has come to provide some additional introspection-based evidence for James's (1890) proposal.

According to ideomotor theory, one is unconscious of the motor efference/events responsible for an action. Hence, experimental participants should introspect that the regions associated with the perceptual consequences of such efference/events are 'where the action is primarily happening' and where the primary generators of the action reside. *Specifically, participants should perceive that the body regions/events associated with the perceptual consequences of an action are more responsible for the action than other regions, even if the other regions are in fact chiefly responsible for causing the action.*

To test this hypothesis, in Experiment 1 we had participants perform simple actions (sniffing, humming, flexing a finger, flexing the arm) and asked them to introspect about the degree to which they believed that certain body regions were responsible for the action. We chose actions that represent the two major body regions—that of the limbs and head-trunk. To not bias participants to focus on only a subset of regions, participants were asked to rate the degree to which every primary body region was responsible for the action. According to ideomotor theory, participants should perceive bodily regions that are most associated with action consequences (e. g. , the nose for sniffing) to be more responsible for an action than regions actually responsible for the action (e. g. , the chest/torso area). For sniffing and humming, participants should believe that the actions are engendered more by the nose and mouth, respectively, than by abdominal sources, even though the latter play an essential role in the constitution of these actions (Tortora 1994). Likewise, regarding finger and arm flexing, participants should believe that the finger tip or a point on the hand, respectively, is more responsible for the action than more proximal muscular regions (e. g. , *m. brachioradialis*), which are responsible for the changes in bodily state (Tortora 1994).

To further investigate introspections about the perceptual consequences of action, we took the opportunity in Experiment 2 to examine lay intuitions regarding simple acts of perceptual inquiry—what it is like to view or touch something for a short period of time.

Together, these studies test an overarching theory about the nature of human action while revealing lay beliefs about the nature of action and perception. It is our hope that these data will complement knowledge of folk beliefs regarding other natural phenomena (cf. , Keil 2003; McCloskey 1983).

EXPERIMENT 1

Methods

Participants. San Francisco State University undergraduate students ($n =$ 108) participated for course credit. These participants have taken at least one course in psychology and may have learned about the actual mechanisms of action production, knowledge which could bias self-reports. If anything, such a bias should lead to data at odds with ideomotor theory.

Procedure. Each participant gave informed consent before participating in the study. Each participant was provided with a paper-and-pencil packet containing instructions for four action tasks as well as pages on which to jot down introspections about the actions. Each of the tasks was a simple everyday action, involving breathing (sniffing, humming) and fine (finger) and gross (arm) movements. In Task 1, participants were asked to "sniff in and out through your nostrils in six quick bursts. " We predicted that participants would believe that the nose region (where action-consequences are felt most) is more responsible for the action than the torso and chest, regions which, like the bag of a bag pipe, are primarily responsible for the passage of air through the nose, an essential component of the action. Likewise, in Task 2, participants were asked to "hum the 'mmmm' sound for four seconds". We predicted that participants would perceive the throat and mouth regions, regions where action-consequences are felt most (and which do participate in action production), to be more responsible for the action than the torso and chest, regions generating the air flow passing through the vocal apparatus and the resonant chambers of the throat (Denes & Pinson 1993). Tasks 3 and 4 involved actions of the hand and arm. To instruct participants to flex the finger without mentioning the body part(s) involved (which would bias participants' responses), for Task 3 participants were instructed to "perform the action that one would perform to spray perfume or cologne in one location on this paper four times". Similarly, to instruct participants to flex their arms without mentioning body parts, for Task 4 participants were instructed to "perform the action that one would perform to raise and lower a hammer four times". We predicted that the finger (Task 3) and hand (Task 4) regions would be perceived as more responsible for the actions than areas of the forearm and upper arm, respectively, even though these areas are critical for generating the actions (Tortora 1994).

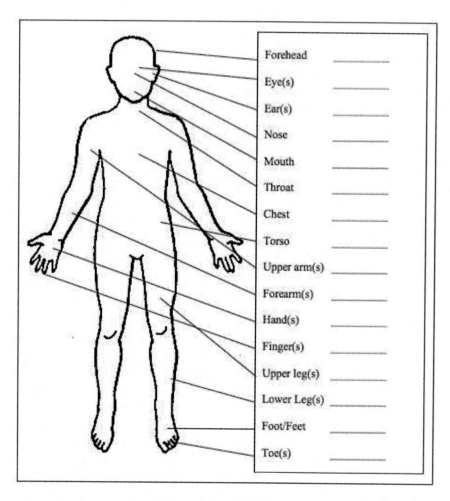

Figure 1. Diagram of the body on which participants rated how responsible they felt each body region was for the action they performed.

Following each task, participants turned to the next page, which displayed a diagram of the human body (Figure 1). On this figure, participants were instructed to "please rate how much you feel each of these regions listed below was responsible for the action on a scale from 1 to 8 (1 = not responsible and 8

= entirely responsible)". Participants were told to "be sure to give a rating for each body part below". It is important to note that, during each task, care was taken to ensure that no reference was made to any body parts, which could bias participants' introspections. In addition, to not bias participants to focus on just a subset of all body regions, participants were asked about the degree to which they felt each body region was responsible for the action. It is important to note that it was emphasized to participants that judgments should be based, not on previously-learned knowledge about action production, but solely on their introspected experience.

Results

As predicted, participants felt that the nose ($M = 7.49$, $SEM = .12$) was significantly more responsible for sniffing than the chest region ($M = 6.67$, $SEM = .17$), $t_{paired}(106) = 4.5$, $p < .0001$, or torso region ($M = 4.92$, $SEM = .25$), $t_{paired}(106) = 10.129$, $p < .0001$. (One participant failed to provide ratings for this task.) In short, the nose was perceived as more responsible for the action than any other region, $ps < .0001$. (Table 1 reveals which contrasts were significant in each of the four tasks.) An omnibus ANOVA on the sniffing-related ratings for all body parts revealed a significant effect of the factor'body region,' $F(15, 1590) = 195.821$, $p < .001$. Similarly, for the humming action, the mouth ($M = 6.40$, $SEM = .22$) and throat ($M = 6.93$, $SEM = .18$) were perceived to be more responsible for the action than the chest ($M = 5.10$, $SEM = .23$) or torso ($M = 3.61$, $SEM = .25$), $ps < .01$, as predicted. (One participant failed to provide ratings for this task.) It is important to note that, as mentioned above, the mouth and throat regions do participate in the production of this action. Thus, participants are accurate in rating that these regions are responsible. What is interesting is that, as for the sniffing task, the areas associated most with the perceptual consequences of the action (e.g., the mouth and throat) were yet again rated as most responsible for the action. An ANOVA on the humming-related ratings for all body parts revealed a significant effect of body region, $F(15, 1575) = 113.66$, $p < .0001$.

Table 1.

| Body Part/Region | Action | | | |
	Sniffing	Humming	Finger Flexion	Arm Flexion
Forehead	2.06 (.17)	2.51 (.22)	1.83 (.17)	1.81 (.16)
Eye(s)	2.43 (.21)	3.16 (.27)	4.78 (.24)	3.83 (.24)
Ear(s)	1.81 (.15)	4.00 (.25)	1.54 (.13)	1.56 (.14)
Nose	7.49 (.12)	4.09 (.26) ⌐	2.07 (.20)	1.38 (.11)
Mouth	3.90 (.25)	6.40 (.22)	1.62 (.15)	1.33 (.11)
Throat	4.90 (.24)	6.93 (.18) ⌐	1.52 (.14)	1.36 (.12)
Chest	**6.67 (.17)** ⌐	5.10 (.23)	1.94 (.18)	2.56 (.20)
Torso	**4.92 (.25)**	3.61 (.25)	1.99 (.18)	2.58 (.20)
Upper Arm(s)	1.61 (.16)	1.64 (.15)	4.74 (.23)	**6.41 (.19)** ⌐
Forearm(s)	1.45 (.13)	1.57 (.15)	5.60 (.21)	**6.96 (.14)**
Hand(s)	1.51 (.15)	1.77 (.18)	6.88 (.18)	**6.90 (.17)** ⌐
Finger(s)	1.50 (.16)	1.86 (.20)	7.28 (.17)	**6.00 (.21)**
Upper Leg(s)	1.31 (.11)	1.37 (.13)	1.27 (.10)	1.38 (.12)
Lower Leg(s)	1.29 (.11)	1.36 (.12)	1.26 (.10)	1.35 (.12)
Foot/Feet	1.36 (.13)	1.40 (.13)	1.21 (.10)	1.35 (.12)
Toe(s)	1.30 (.12)	1.38 (.13)	1.19 (.09)	1.31 (.11)

Note. Mean rating of how responsible participants felt each region of the body was for the actions they performed. Ratings stem from a 1-8 scale, in which 1 = "not responsible at all" and 8 = "entirely responsible." Bold font indicates regions of interest for that particular task. Brackets denote contrasts within the critical region that are non-significant ($ps > .05$). The table reports the mean rating of how responsible on a 1-8 (1 = not responsible at all, 8 = entirely responsible) scale participants felt each region of the body was for the actions they performed. *SEM*s are presented in parentheses.

For finger flexing, participants rated the finger ($M = 7.28$, $SEM = .17$) as more responsible for the flexing action than one of the primary anatomical sources of the action, the forearm ($M = 5.60$, $SEM = .21$), $t_{paired} (107) = 8.69$, $p < .001$. An ANOVA on the finger-flexion ratings for all body parts revealed a significant effect of body region, $F (15, 1590) = 226.234$ $p < .0001$. Similarly, for arm flexing, participants rated the hand ($M = 6.90$, $SEM = .17$) as significantly more responsible for the action than one of the primary anatomical sources of the action, the upper arm ($M = 6.41$, $SEM = .19$), $t (107) = 2.72$, $p < .01$. An omnibus ANOVA on the arm-flexion ratings for all body parts revealed a significant effect of body region, $F (15, 1605) = 305.35$, $p < .0001$.

EXPERIMENT 2

To further investigate introspections about the perceptual consequences of action, in Experiment 2 we examined the same participants' lay intuitions regarding the afference resulting from simple acts of perceptual inquiry. This study was inspired by Frijda's (2001) astute observation that one's intuition of what it feels like to see or touch something is quite different from what one actually introspects when performing the act (similar claims are found in Lotze 1852; James 1890).

Methods

Procedure. Using the same kinds of materials as Experiment 1, the experiment consisted of two introspection tasks involving basic perceptual acts, one involving vision (staring at a pattern for 30 sec) and one involving touch (touching a surface). To learn about initial views regarding the sensory experience, a question preceded each of the tasks. For the visual task, participants were first asked, "without performing this task, how strongly do you feel on a scale from 1 to 8 (1 = not strong at all, and 8 = very strongly) that you know what it is like to stare at an image for 30 seconds?" After indicating their rating, participants were instructed to stare at an image of a square containing nine dots (Figure 2) for 30 sec. The figure did not feature an illusion of any sort. After staring at the image for 30 sec, participants were asked "while you performed this task, how different was your experience from what you expected on a 1 to 8 scale? (1 = not different at all, and 8 = very different). " Participants were then provided with the opportunity to write down in an open-ended manner the way in which their experience differed from what was expected.

For Task 2 (touching something with the finger tip), participants were first asked to rate, "without performing this task how strongly do you feel on a scale from 1 to 8 (1 = not strong at all, and 8 = very strongly) that you know what it feels like to touch something with your fingertip?" Next, participants were instructed to touch with their fingertip the inside of a circle printed on the page. They were then asked the same two questions that followed Task 1.

QuickTime™ and a
decompressor
are needed to see this picture.

Figure 2. Image participants were instructed to stare at for 30 sec in Experiment 2.

Results

For the visual task, participants' mean initial judgment about how well they knew what it is like to stare at an object for 30 seconds was 6. 03 (*SEM* = . 17). (One participant provided no ratings.) After staring at the image for 30 seconds, participants' average rating for how different their experience was from expected was 3. 84 (*SEM* = . 22). A single sample t-test revealed that participants' experience (M = 3. 84) was significantly different from 1, the value signifying that the experience was no different from what was anticipated, t (106) = 13. 21, p < . 001. Regarding the nature of the experience, participants reported that the unanticipated aspect of the experience involved changes that were perceptual (n = 21 [19. 6%] of 107), attentional (8 [7. 5%]), time-perception related (7 [6. 5%]), eye movement-based (6 [5. 6%]), or'miscellaneous' (13 [12. 1%]). (Fifty-two [48. 5%] provided no response.) Two judges agreed 100% about this classification of participants' open-ended responses. See Table 2 for a sample of participants' intriguing introspections about Tasks 1 and 2.

For Task 2, participants' initial judgment about how well they knew what it is like to touch something with their fingertip was 6. 90 (*SEM* = . 13). After performing the action, introspections regarding how different their experience was 2. 52 (*SEM* = . 21). A single sample t-test revealed that participants' experience (M = 2. 52) was significantly greater than 1, t(107) = 7. 08, p < . 001. Participants reported that the unanticipated aspect of the experience involved changes that were perceptual (n = 18 [16. 7%] of 108) or'miscellaneous' (13 [12. 0%]). (Seventy-seven [71. 3%] provided no response.) Two judges agreed 100% about this classification of participants' striking open-ended responses.

Together, the findings from Experiment 2 corroborate Frijda's (2001) observation that our lay intuitions about perceptual acts do not fully capture that which unfolds when performing those acts.

Table 2. Sample introspections about unanticipated perceptual changes during Tasks 1 (staring at a pattern) and 2 (touching a surface)

Task 1

1. I shifted from circle to circle and it appeared as though some of the circles were popping out while others were not.
2. I thought I was just going to be staring at a same size dots but as I focused more it seemed as if some of the dots were increasing in size.
3. My perception of the object kept shifting and I couldn't focus on the object as a whole very well.
4. After a while the dots began to gain shadows as if the dots were not crisp circles. I didn't expect that.
5. Saw patterns in the dots.
6. You lose meaning of what you are looking at after a while and it feels so much longer.
7. I thought the image would remain consistent for 30 sec, but the circles kept on getting bigger and smaller.
8. The image seemed to become more distorted while staring at it. I expected the image to remain pretty much the same throughout the timeframe.
9. The dots seemed to float at times. At first I was focused on the whole image but as the time went by different patterns in the groups of dots seemed to stand out at different times.

Task 2

1. I didn't feel the paper as much as I thought I would.
2. It was a little different because I was more in tuned to exactly how much of my fingertip was on the paper. I never thought of that before.
3. There is not as much sensation as I anticipated from just touching. It is different than stroking.
4. What I imagined is pressure on my finger tip when touch was a bit less than how it really felt.
5. It was different because I believed I was going to feel more than I did and I

imagined that what I was touching was more course than what I actually felt.

6. Less sensation than initially anticipated.

DISCUSSION

Only recently has research begun to focus on the basic mechanisms in action production (Hommel et al. 2001; Nattkemper & Ziessler 2004). Although widely held to be true, aspects of ideomotor theory have never been examined empirically. Consistent with the ideomotor principle, in Experiment 1 the nose was felt to be more responsible for sniffing than the chest or torso. This is quite striking when one considers that the tissues of the nose (e. g. , cartilage) cannot really'do much,' because they receive little if any efference. In general, participants believed that bodily processes associated with the perceptual consequences of action-related efference/events were more responsible for actions than, in some cases, the actual anatomical sources of the actions. Participants' knowledge about the true mechanics underlying action production could have influenced the judgments. However, if anything, such knowledge should have led to an opposite pattern of results, such as that it is the chest/torso region that is primarily responsible for sniffing.

Extending the research into the realm of perceptual acts, Experiment 2 provides initial evidence for the counter-intuitive view that people are less aware of what it is like to introspect a perceptual event over a short period of time. More generally, the findings of Experiment 2 are consistent with mounting evidence showing that people tend to overestimate how much they actually know about the nature of their everyday perceptual experiences (e. g. , as in *change blindness*; Simons & Levin 1997) and that people are inaccurate at predicting the nature of future subjective states (e. g. , as in *affective forecasting*; Wilson & Gilbert 2005).

Beyond serving as additional, citable evidence for one of the main tenets of ideomotor theory (Greenwald 1970; James 1890; Hommel 2009; Hommel & Elsner 2009; Hommel et al. 2001), it is our hope that these data will complement knowledge of lay beliefs regarding other natural phenomena (e. g. , Keil 2003).

REFERENCES

Ach, N. (1905/1951). Determining tendencies: Awareness. In D. Rapaport (Ed.), *Organization and pathology of thought* (pp. 15-38). New York: Columbia University Press. (Original work published in 1905).

Agnew, C. R. , Carlston, D. E. , Graziano, W. G. , & Kelly, J. R. (2009). *Then a miracle occurs: Focusing on behavior in social psychological theory and research*. New York: Oxford University Press.

Carpenter, W. B. (1874). *Principles of mental physiology*. New York: Appleton.

Denes, P. , & Pinson, E. (1993). The speech chain: The physics and biology of spoken language. New York: Worth Publishers.

Frijda, N. H. (2001). The nature of pleasure. In J. A. Bargh and D. K. Apsley (Eds.), *Unraveling the complexities of social life: A Festschrift in honor of Robert B. Zajonc* (pp. 71-94). Washington, DC: American Psychological Association.

Gray, J. A. (1995). The contents of consciousness: A neuropsychological conjecture. *Behavioral and Brain Sciences 18,* 659-676.

Gray, J. A. (2004). *Consciousness: Creeping up on the hard problem.* New York: Oxford University Press.

Greenwald, A. G. (1970). Sensory feedback mechanisms in performance control: With special reference to the ideomotor mechanism. *Psychological Review, 77,* 73-99.

Grossberg, S. (1999). The link between brain learning, attention, and consciousness. *Consciousness and Cognition, 8,* 1-44.

Harleß, E. (1861). *Der Apparat des Willens. Zeitschrift für Philosophie und philosophische Kritik, 38,* 499-507.

Hommel, B. (2009). Action control according to TEC (theory of event coding). *Psychological Research, 73,* 512-526.

Hommel, B. , & Elsner, B. (2009). Acquisition, representation, and control of action. In E. Morsella, J. A. Bargh, & P. M. Gollwitzer (eds.), *Oxford handbook of human action* (pp. 371-398). New York: Oxford University Press.

Hommel, B. , Müsseler, J. , Aschersleben, G. , & Prinz, W. (2001). The theory of event coding: A framework for perception and action planning. *Behavioral and Brain Sciences, 24,* 849-937.

James, W. (1890). *Principles of Psychology.* New York: Holt.

Jeannerod, M. (2006). *Motor cognition: What action tells the self.* New York: Oxford University Press.

Keil, F. C. (2003). Folkscience: Coarse interpretations of a complex reality. *Trends in Cognitive Science, 7,* 368-373.

Klein, D. B. (1970). *A history of scientific psychology: Its origins and philosophical backgrounds.* New York: Basic Books.

Lotze, R. H. (1852). *Medizinische Psychologie oder Physiologie der Seele.* Leipzig: Weidmann'sche Buchhandlung.

McCloskey, M. (1983). Intuitive physics. *Scientific American, 248,* 122-130.

Melcher, T. , Weidema, M. , Eenshuistra, R. M. , Hommel, B. , & Gruber, O. (2008). The neural substrate of the ideomotor principle: An event-related fMRI analysis. *NeuroImage, 39,* 1274-1288.

Morsella, E. (2009). The mechanisms of human action: Introduction and background. In E. Morsella, J. A. Bargh, & P. M. Gollwitzer, *Oxford handbook of human action* (pp. 1-32). New York: Oxford University Press.

Nattkemper, D. , & Ziessler, M. (2004): Editorial: Cognitive control of action: The role of action effects. *Psychological Research, 68,* 71-73.

Rosenbaum, D. A. (2002). Motor control. In H. Pashler (Series Ed.) & S. Yantis (Vol. Ed.), *Stevens' handbook of experimental psychology: Vol. 1. Sensation and perception* (3rd ed. , pp. 315-339). New York: Wiley.

Rossetti, Y. (2001). Implicit perception in action: Short-lived motor representation of space. In P. G. Grossenbacher (Ed.), *Finding consciousness in the brain: A neurocognitive approach* (pp. 133-181). Netherlands: John Benjamins Publishing.

Scheerer, E. (1987). Muscle sense and innervation feelings: A chapter in the history of perception and action. In H. Heuer A. F. Sanders (Eds.), *Perspectives of Perception and action* (pp. 171-194). Hillsdale, NJ: Lawrence Erlbaum.

Simons, D. J. , & Levin, D. T. (1997). Change blindness. *Trends in Cognitive Sciences, 1,* 261-267.

Tortora, G. J. (1994). *Introduction to the human body: The essentials of anatomy and physiology, third edition.* New York: Harper Collins.

Wegner, D. M. (2002). *The illusion of conscious will.* Cambridge, MA: MIT Press.

Wegner, D. M. (2003). The mind's best trick: How we experience conscious will. *Trends in Cognitive Science, 7,* 65-69.

Wilson, T. D. , & Gilbert, D. T. (2005). Affective forecasting: Knowing what to want. *Current Directions in Psychological Science, 14,* 131-134.

Woodworth, R. S. (1939). The cause of a voluntary movement. *Psychological Issues: Selected Papers of Robert S. Woodworth.* New York: Columbia University Press.

In: Psychology of Self-Control
Editors: A. Durante, et. al.

ISBN: 978-1-61470-881-0
© 2012 Nova Science Publishers, Inc.

Chapter 7

THE SELF-MANAGEMENT CORRELATES OF SOCIAL ANXIETY

Alexander M. Penney[1], Peter G. Mezo[2]
[1]Memorial University of Newfoundland, Canada
[2]Memorial University of Newfoundland, Canada

Abstract

Self-control or self-management (Kanfer, 1970; Mezo, 2009) is composed of three interdependent constructs: self-monitoring (SM), self-evaluating (SE), and self-reinforcing (SR). To date, a self-management model for anxiety does not exist. Forty-five undergraduate students completed the Self-Control and Self-Management Scale (SCMS; Mezo, 2009), three measures of social anxiety, and a social desirability measure. As predicted, SM, SE and total SCMS scores negatively correlated with the social anxiety measures. Using a diagnostically valid cutoff score, the participants were divided into low and high anxiety groups. Independent t-tests revealed that the high anxiety group had significant deficits in overall self-management, and significant deficits in SE relative to the low anxiety group. The role of these results in the development of a self-management model for anxiety, along with limitations and possibilities for future research, are discussed.

Self-management, also referred to as self-control (Kanfer, 1970; Kanfer & Karoly, 1972), is the use of self-administered reinforcement and punishment to strengthen chosen behaviours, without relying on environmental contingencies. Self-management is composed of three interdependent constructs: self-monitoring (SM), self-evaluating (SE), and self-reinforcing (SR). During SM the individual monitors his or her own behaviours and thoughts in terms of a selected goal. In the SE phase, the individual compares these actions against personal standards to determine any discrepancies. Based on this evaluation, the individual applies SR, which can be either self-reward or self-punishment, and may be overt or covert. The outcome of SR feeds back into SM, thus influencing whether self-management will be continued, changed, or abandoned.

Deficient self-management has been associated with a variety of problems, particularly depression (Rehm, 1977). Self-control therapy that targets SM, SE, and SR (see Fuchs & Rehm, 1977) is listed as one of the probably efficacious treatments for depression in the empirically validated therapies report by Chambless and colleagues (1998). In Rehm's (1977; Fuchs & Rehm, 1977) model of depression, individuals with depression exhibit two deficits in each of the three components of self-management. When engaging in SM, people with depression focus on the immediate outcomes of their actions, without noticing long term goals, as they focus selectively on negative events. During SE, people with depression make incorrect internal attributions of causality, and set perfectionist and unrealistic goals for themselves. When engaged in SR, depressed people exhibit low rates of self-reward and very high rates of self-punishment.

Due to the effectiveness self-management therapy for depression, the possibility of a self-management therapy for anxiety ought to be considered. It is important to note that depression and anxiety have been found to share the underlying construct of negative affectivity (Watson et al. , 1995). Thus, with negative affect being common to all emotional disorders, and symptom structures overlapping among disorders, developing unified treatments for all mood disorders have been considered (Barlow, Allen, & Choate, 2004).

Kanfer and Schefft (1988) remark that a general rule of self-management therapy is to see anxiety as a cue for intervention. In the past, treatments have utilized self-management principles for treating agoraphobia and social anxiety, but have done so without an overarching self-management model of anxiety. In treatments of agoraphobia, both Taylor (1985) and Emmelkamp (1974) focused on increasing SM. Emmelkamp (1974) further instructed participants to increase behaviours that increased anxiety, and to engage in SM of the anxiety during this time. This treatment was found to be as effective as treatment via flooding (Emmelkamp, 1974). Rehm and Marston (1968) developed a treatment for social phobia centered on SR, but because SR requires input from SM, the treatment increased SM as well. The therapy, developed for socially anxious men, involved creating a desensitization hierarchy for social interactions. When participants completed a task in a given week, they awarded themselves points for meeting the requirements of the task and additional points for going beyond what was expected. Therapists encouraged awarding more points, but did not suggest new behaviours. After five weeks, participants were much less socially anxious than a non-directive therapy group, or a waitlist control group. Therefore, while therapies for anxiety using self-management are effective, no comprehensive model of anxiety has been developed based on self-management.

This study explored a conceptual background for a new self-management model of anxiety. A variety of self-management instruments have been correlated to anxiety in previous studies, but only general anxiety measures have been used (Mezo, 2009; Mezo & Heiby, 2004). More specifically, Mezo & Heiby (2004) found that four self-management instruments all correlated negatively with a general measure of anxiety, indicating that people with higher anxiety were often worse at engaging in self-management. However, these self-management instruments were not designed to measure SM, SE and SR as separable facets of the self-management construct. In contrast, the Self-Control and Self-Management Scale (SCMS; Mezo, 2009) was designed to measure each self-management facet. When the SCMS was correlated to a general measure of anxiety, the overall score, along with the SE and SR subscale scores, negatively correlated to anxiety, but the SM subscale score did not (Mezo, 2009). To further evaluate the manner in which self-management and anxiety relate, the correlates of the self-management components to specific anxiety disorders ought to be explored. One such disorder is social anxiety disorder.

Social anxiety disorder is defined in the DSM-IV (American Psychiatric Association, 1994) as a marked and persistent fear of one or more social or performance situations, in which the person is exposed to unfamiliar people or to possible scrutiny by others. The individual fears that he or she will act in a way (or show anxiety symptoms) that will be humiliating or embarrassing. In recent community samples, lifetime prevalence in Western countries of social anxiety disorder ranges from 7-13% (Furmark, 2002). However, there is considerable variation amongst prevalence estimates. Issues such as diagnostic criteria, diagnostic threshold, and cultural norms all play important roles in this variability. Onset of social anxiety often occurs in childhood or early adolescence, with a chronic and unremitting course. As the person ages, the impairment continues to restrict their social interaction, which further increases their functional impairment. This iterative, vicious cycle of avoidant social behaviours and social withdrawal and alienation can profoundly deteriorate quality of life over the lifecourse (Belzer, McKee, & Liebowitz, 2005).

In current psychological treatments for social anxiety disorder there is an emphasis on the use of fear hierarchies and cognitive restructuring (Belzer et al. , 2005). Although these treatments are quite effective, their efficacy can be interpreted through various cognitive-behavioural models, including a self-management model. Working through fear hierarchies, while distressing for the clients, significantly changes the way the clients administer SR. Instead of punishing themselves for acting irrationally in public, they now reward themselves for doing such actions and allowing the anxiety to subside. With cognitive restructuring, the SE changes from thoughts of inadequacy and failure, to thoughts of achievement and success. In both techniques, the SM has been transformed from a focus on external social stimuli and internal anxiety, to a more broad based monitoring of internal and external events. Such an analysis illustrates not only that it is possible for self-management theory to characterize treatment mechanisms in social anxiety disorder, but it also suggests that self-management theory can produce clinical hypotheses so as to identify key social deficits that may be targeted in therapy.

To begin to identify possible self-management deficits in people with social anxiety, the correlations between overall self-management, as well as all three facets of self-management, and social anxiety were investigated in the current study. It was hypothesized that both overall self-management, as well as the three facets of self-management, would attain significant, moderate negative correlations with social anxiety. Moreover, it was hypothesized that people with social anxiety scores that are comparable to those diagnosed with social anxiety disorder would have lower scores on total self-management and on the three facets of self-management than people with lower social anxiety scores. These results would help provide preliminary support for the continued elaboration of a self-management of social anxiety disorder.

METHOD

Participants

The sample for this study was drawn from undergraduate students at Memorial University of Newfoundland who were enrolled in Introductory Psychology. In total, 45 students completed the study, of which 36 (80%) were women. Nevertheless, sex was not found to significantly correlate to any of the measures used in the study. Ages ranged from 18 to 22, and 43 students identified themselves as Euro-American. Students originated from nine different faculties at Memorial University of Newfoundland, with Arts ($n = 16$), Science ($n = 7$), and Education ($n = 6$) faculties most heavily represented.

Procedure

Following ethical approval from the Interdisciplinary Committee on Ethics in Human Research, volunteers were recruited from Introductory Psychology. A brief description of the study was presented to each class, followed by the circulation of a contact information sheet. Students who chose to volunteer wrote down their contact information and were contacted via email within four weeks. The participants provided informed consent before completing the study. Participants were entered into a draw for one of five $10 gift certificates.

Based on scheduling availability, participants were scheduled in groups, to a maximum of five people per group. Participants were given four self-report instruments to complete. Instrument order was counterbalanced using the Latin square technique. A demographics questionnaire was also included. The self-report instruments utilized in this study were the Marlowe-Crowne Social Desirability Scale (MCS; Crowne & Marlowe, 1960), the Self-Control and Self-Management Scale (SCMS; Mezo, 2009), the Social Interaction Anxiety Scale and Social Phobia Scale (SIAS and SPS; Mattick & Clarke, 1998), and the Social Phobia Inventory (SPIN; Connor et al. , 2000). The time to complete the study measures was approximately 30 minutes for each participant.

Measures

The MCS (Crowne & Marlowe, 1960) is a 33-item true/false questionnaire designed to measure a participant's response bias towards socially desirable responses. Scores can range from 0 to 33.

The SCMS (Mezo, 2009) is a 16-item questionnaire designed to measure self-management, with items scored on a six-point Likert scale. Scores can range from 0 to 80. The SCMS consists of a SM subscale, a SE subscale, and a SR subscale. The SCMS has been shown to have high content validity (well defined three factor structure, with moderate subscale intercorrelations), and high internal consistency and stability reliability in an undergraduate sample (Mezo, 2009).

The SIAS (Mattick & Clarke, 1998) and SPS (Mattick & Clarke, 1998) are complementary measures of fears of social interaction (as measured by the SIAS), and fears of being scrutinized (as measured by the SPS). Both consist of 20 items, and are scored on five-point Likert scales. Scores can range from 0 to 80 on both measures. Both the SIAS and SPS have shown high internal consistency and stability reliability, and strong convergent and divergent validity in both clinical and nonclinical samples (Orsillo, 2001).

The SPIN (Connor et al. , 2000) is a 17-item measure, scored on a five-point Likert scale, and scores can range from 0 to 68. The SPIN's three subscales are Fear, Avoidance, and Physiological Arousal. Internal consistency across the overall instrument and subscales ranged from moderate to high, with high stability reliability. Strong convergent and discriminant validity has been found, and a cutoff score of 19 has distinguished between individuals with or without a diagnosis of social anxiety disorder (79% diagnostic efficiency; Orsillo, 2001).

RESULTS

The mean scores and score distributions for all instruments were adequate to allow for further analyses: MCS ($M = 15. 67$, $SD = 4. 54$), SCMS ($M = 58. 71$, $SD = 10. 92$), SPS ($M = 20. 42$, $SD = 13. 23$), SIAS ($M = 26. 53$, $SD = 13. 05$), and SPIN ($M = 20. 73$, $SD = 11. 47$). Bivariate correlations were obtained between the total scores on the SCMS, the total scores on the MCS, and the total scores of the anxiety measures (see Table 1). It is notable that the MCS score significantly correlated to the total scores on all measures. However, no participants achieved extreme scores of social desirability (i. e. , scores three standard deviations above the mean on the MCS). Bivariate correlations were also conducted between the SCMS total scores, SCMS subscale scores, the SPS scores, the SIAS scores, the SPIN total scores, and SPIN subscale scores (see Table 2). Both the SCMS total score and SE subscale correlated significantly and negatively with all social anxiety measures. The SM subscale correlated significantly and negatively to the SIAS, the SPIN total score, and both of the SPIN fear and avoidance subscales. Finally, the SR subscale correlated significantly and negatively to the SIAS.

Table 1. Bivariate Correlations between the Marlowe-Crowne Social Desirability Scale (MCS), the Self-Control and Self-Management Scale (SCMS), the Social Phobia Scale (SPS), the Social Interaction Anxiety Scale (SIAS), and the Social Phobia Inventory (SPIN)

	MCS	SCMS	SPS	SIAS
SCMS	. 427**	-		
SPS	-. 545**	-. 313*	-	
SIAS	-. 486**	-. 562**	. 728**	-
SPIN	-. 516**	-. 478**	. 834**	. 839**

*$p < . 05$.
**$p < . 01$.

Next, the participants were divided into two groups on the basis of the SPIN clinical cutoff score of 19. Participants scoring 19 or above are considered to be comparable to clinically socially anxious individuals in terms of social anxiety (Orsillo, 2001). In total, 24 of the 45 participants satisfied this criterion. Using independent t-tests, it was found that the total SCMS scores were lower in the high social anxiety group ($M = 55. 13$, $SD = 12. 62$) than the low social anxiety group ($M = 62. 81$, $SD = 6. 77$), $t(43) = 2. 49$, $p = . 017$. Scores on the SE subscale were also significantly lower in the high social anxiety group ($M = 17. 04$, $SD = 6. 57$) than in the low social anxiety group ($M = 21. 05$, $SD = 3. 29$), $t(43) = 2. 53$, $p = . 015$. No other differences between the groups emerged.

Table 2. Bivariate correlations between the Self-Control and Self-Management Scale (SCMS) total score, Self-Monitoring subscale (SM), Self-Evaluating subscale (SE), Self-Reinforcing subscale (SR), the Social Phobia Scale (SPS), the Social Interaction Anxiety Scale (SIAS), the Social Phobia Inventory (SPIN) total score, Fear subscale (FEAR), Avoidance subscale (AVO) and Physiological Arousal subscale (PHY)

	SCMS	SM	SE	SR	SPS	SIAS	SPIN	FEAR	AVO
SM	.849**	-							
SE	.900**	.692**	-						
SR	.629**	.311*	.352*	-					
SPS	-.313*	-.228	-.441**	.010	-				
SIAS	-.562**	-.361*	-.572**	-.388**	.728**	-			
SPIN	-.478**	-.336*	-.533**	-.220	.834**	.839**	-		
FEAR	-.450**	-.307*	-.543**	-.155	.825**	.827**	.953**	-	
AVO	-.488**	-.324*	-.537**	-.260	.733**	.826**	.934**	.855**	-
PHY	-.313*	-.266	-.309*	-.154	.699**	.554**	.790**	.694**	.563**

*p < .05.
**p < .01.

DISCUSSION

This study sought to examine the relevance of the self-management theoretical model (Kanfer, 1970; Kanfer & Karoly, 1972; Mezo, 2009) to social anxiety. Although self-management strategies have been utilized to treat anxiety in the past (Taylor, 1985; Emmelkamp, 1974; Rehm & Marston, 1968), no overriding self-management model of anxiety has been established. Without a cohesive theoretical model, self-management therapies for this class of disorders may not be as effectively developed in the future. If people with anxiety are found to express key limitations in terms of self-management, these limitations may then become specific targets for therapy. The results of the current study begin to illuminate the roles of self-monitoring (SM), self-evaluating (SE) and overall self-management in the context of social anxiety.

Contrary to the original hypotheses, not all facets of self-management correlated significantly with social anxiety. As indicated by scores on the Self-Control and Self-Management Scale (SCMS; Mezo, 2009), the SCMS total score and the SE subscale were found to correlate with all of the social anxiety measures. Also, the SM subscale correlated significantly to all social anxiety measures, with the exceptions of the Social Phobia Scale (SPS; Mattick & Clarke, 1998), and the Social Phobia Inventory (SPIN; Connor et al. , 2000) Physiological Arousal subscale. However, the Self-Reinforcing (SR) subscale was found to significantly correlate with only the Social Interaction Anxiety Scale (SIAS; Mattick & Clarke, 1998) total score. These findings suggest that overall self-management, and specifically SM and SE, are possibly more important factors in social anxiety than SR is. When participants were divided into high social anxiety and low social anxiety groups on the basis of the SPIN cutoff score, results again revealed differences in SE and general self-management. The high anxiety group showed significantly lower mean scores on both the SE subscale and the SCMS total scores than the low anxiety group. As there were no differences found between the groups on the SM or SR subscales, it appears that deficits in SE may be particularly important with regard to social anxiety and suggests that SE may be the largest contributor to social anxiety of the three components of self-management.

As discussed earlier, anxiety and depression share the common emotional dimension of high negative affectivity (Watson et al. , 1995). Similarly, the commonality of anxiety and depression has fostered ongoing research on unified treatment protocols for these disorders (Barlow et al. , 2004). From these perspectives, perhaps due to a common emotional vulnerability, the self-management components of SM and SE appear to be important factors in both anxiety and depression. More specifically, although the targets of monitoring or evaluation may differ somewhat in anxiety versus depression, the processes appear to dovetail. As an example of SM in both anxiety and depression, individuals with social anxiety disorder are quite likely to be monitoring not only their own actions, so as to ensure social competence, but also the actions of others, so as to detect social disapproval (Belzer et al. , 2005). Likewise, individuals with depression are likely to be monitoring for current personal failures, with a disregard or de-emphasis on a long-term goals and a broader view of life circumstances (Rehm, 1977). From a self-regulatory perspective, engaging in either of these processes repeatedly and over time can lead to a cascade of deepening symptomatology, either social anxiety or depression, and an emotional inertia from which it is exceedingly difficult for an individual to extricate oneself.

Nevertheless, anxiety and depression also have significant differences. At the broad, emotion level, anxiety does not appear to have deficits in positive affect, but low positive affect is a cardinal feature of depression (Watson et al. , 1995). This difference between anxiety and depression may help account for the observed lack of effect of SR on social anxiety in this study. Deficits in SR have been shown to be important predictions of depressed mood, and are thought to help maintain depression (Heiby, 1982). It may be that SR is one of the mechanisms through which anhedonia, and low positive affect more generally, is augmented. However, it is important to keep in mind that SM, SE, and SR are interdependent constructs, making up self-management as a whole. Problems in any one of the three components of self-management may be expected to cause irregularities in self-management overall. Indeed, deficits in overall self-management of socially anxious individuals were uncovered in this study.

Given the preliminary findings of this study, it is worthwhile to continue research into the nature of the SM and SE deficits in the self-management of socially anxious individuals. The obtained correlations do not mean that the lowered SM and SE of socially anxious individuals cause their social anxiety. However, in light of these findings, targeting SM and SE in therapy for anxious individuals should be considered. For example, in Rehm and Marston's (1968) therapy for socially anxious men, the researchers developed the therapy to increase positive SR. However, due to the interdependence of self-management, it is likely that this therapy increased SM and SE as well. Accordingly, it is possible the men in the experimental condition were now SM for targets other than social mistakes. Likewise, to apply more positive

SR, participants likely evaluated their actions more positively and flexibly (consistent with effective SE). This would have been a dramatic change for these participants, for they would have been more accustomed to noticing their anxiety and mistakes in social situations, rather than their positive actions. Thus, it may have been the change in SM and SE, not SR, which led to treatment gains. Also, cognitive restructuring techniques often used for reducing anxiety may represent a tactic for building SE skills (Rehm & Marston, 1968), rather than changing how one reinforces his or her self. It is for such reasons that a self-management model of social anxiety is needed.

A possible limitation of this study is the correlation found between the SCMS and the Marlowe-Crowne Social Desirability Scale (MCS; Crowne & Marlowe, 1960). While this correlation was unexpected, as the SCMS had previously not significantly correlated to the MCS (Mezo, 2009), it is not without explanation. The SCMS was purposively designed to be conceptually different than social desirability, so that it would not be measuring it. However, this does not mean the SCMS cannot correlate with the MCS. Indeed, although the scores on the SMCS and MCS may covary, this does not indicate that the SCMS is measuring social desirability, anymore than it means the MCS is measuring self-management. As well, the MCS correlated as strongly, if not stronger, to the measures of social anxiety. Therefore, it would appear that the correlations are due to the current sample or the population it represented. The relatively small sample size and use of volunteers likely played key roles in this regard. Moreover, it may be that the population of psychology students behaves in more socially desirable ways, or at least portrays itself that way.

Beyond the possible influence of social desirability, other limitations to the generalizability of this study's results are present. First the participants were largely Euro-American women. The sample also appeared highly anxious, with a mean score above the cutoff of the SPIN. It would appear that mentioning that the study was examining anxiety, or testing people in groups, led to the prevalence of social anxiety being greater than expected norms. As well, because this was a correlational study, it is not definite that issues with SM, SE, or self-management as a whole led to social anxiety. It is possible that social anxiety led to the deficits, or some third factor is influencing the correlations. Finally, the roles of self-efficacy (Bandura, 1991) and other self-management subskills, such as goal formation (Kanfer & Schefft, 1988), were not evaluated. Both self-efficacy and the self-management subskills have been widely discussed in the literature as possible factors in the expression of self-management, and these related constructs may have a significant role to play in the formation of any self-management model of social anxiety.

The results of this investigation point to multiple paths for future research. It is crucial that the sample size of the current study be increased to ensure the correlations found hold true with larger samples. Following replication, a more detailed analysis of SM and SE in socially anxious individuals would need to be completed. Such research could pinpoint what deficits or differences may be causing or maintaining the anxiety. Similarly, replications are also necessary to examine the correlations between self-management, its components, and other anxiety disorders. If SM and SE are found to correlate to the other specific anxiety disorders, a self-management model and therapy for all anxiety disorders could be established. Differences in SM and deficits in SE could represent new mechanisms of change for the treatment of anxiety disorders.

To conclude, self-management therapy has proven to be immensely successful in treating depression, and has been applied to the treatment of anxiety. However, a self-management model for anxiety is lacking, and treatment advances may be stifled without such a model. The present study revealed that, at least for social anxiety, differences in SM and deficits in SE and overall self-management skills may play a causal role in anxiety. With continued research, a complete self-management model for anxiety may be developed.

REFERENCES

American Psychiatric Association (1994). *Diagnostic and statistical manual of mental disorders, 4th edition.* Washington DC, American Psychiatric Association.

Bandura, A. (1991). Social cognitive theory of self-regulation. *Organizational Behavior and Human Decision* Processes, 50, 248-287.

Barlow, D. H. , Allen, L. B. , & Choate, M. L. (2004). Toward a unified treatment for emotional disorders. *Behavior Therapy, 35,* 205-230.

Belzer, K. D. , McKee, M. B. , & Liebowitz, M. R. (2005). Social anxiety disorder: Current perspectives on diagnosis and treatment. *Primary Psychiatry, 12,* 35-48.

Chambless, D. L. , Baker, M. J. , Baucom, D. H. , Beutler, L. E. , Calhoun, K. S. , Crits-Cristoph, P. , et al. (1998). Update on empirically validated therapies, II. *The Clinical Psychologist, 51*, 3-16.

Connor, K. M. , Davidson, J. R. , Churchill, L. E. , Sherwood, A. , Foa, E. , & Weisler, R. H. (2000). Psychometric properties of the social phobia inventory (SPIN): New self-rating scale. *British Journal of Psychiatry, 176*, 379-386.

Crowne, D. P. , & Marlowe, D. (1960). A new scale of social desirability independent of psychopathology. *Journal of Consulting Psychology, 24*, 349-354.

Emmelkamp, P. M. (1974). Self-observation versus flooding in the treatment of agoraphobia. *Behaviour Research and Therapy, 12*, 229-237.

Fuchs, C. Z. , & Rehm, L. P. (1977). A self-control behavior therapy program for depression. *Journal of Consulting and Clinical Psychology, 45*, 206-215.

Furmark, T (2002). Social phobia: Overview of community surveys. *Acta Psychiatrica Scandinavica, 105*, 84-93.

Heiby, E. M. (1982). A self-reinforcement questionnaire. *Behaviour Research and Therapy, 20*, 397-401.

Kanfer, F. H. (1970). Self-regulation: Research, issues, and speculations. In C. Neuringer, & J. L. Michael (Eds.), *Behavior modification in clinical psychology* (pp. 178- 220). New York: Appleton-Century-Crofts.

Kanfer, F. H. , & Karoly, P. (1972). Self-control: A behavioristic excursion into the lion's den. *Behavior Therapy, 3*, 398-416.

Kanfer, F. H. , & Schefft, B. K. (1988). *Guiding the process of therapeutic change*. Champaign, IL: Research Press.

Mattick, R. P. , Clarke, J. C. (1998). Development and validation of measures of social phobia scrutiny fear and social interaction anxiety. *Behaviour Research and Therapy, 36*, 455-470.

Mezo, P. G. (2009). The Self-Control and Self-Management Scale (SCMS): Development of an adaptive self-regulatory coping skills instrument. *Journal of Psychopathology and Behavioral Assessment, 31*, 83-93.

Mezo, P. G. , & Heiby, E. M. (2004). A comparison of four measures of self-control skills. *Assessment, 11,* 238-250.

Orsillo, S. M. (2001). Measures for social phobia. In M. M. Antony, S. M. Orsillo, & L. Roemer (Eds.), *Practitioner's guide to empirically based measures of anxiety.* New York: Kluwer Academic/Plenum Publishers.

Rehm, L. P. (1977). A self-control model of depression. *Behavior Therapy, 8,* 787-804.

Rehm, L. P. , & Marston, A. R. (1968). Reduction of social anxiety through modification of self-reinforcement: An instigation therapy technique. *Journal of Consulting and Clinical Psychology, 32,* 565-574.

Taylor, I. (1985). The reactive effects of self-monitoring of target activities in agoraphobia: A pilot study. *Scandinavian Journal of Behaviour Therapy, 14,* 17-22.

Watson, D. , Clark, L. A. , Weber, K. , Assenheimer, J. S. , Strauss, M. E. , McCormick, R. A. (1995). Testing a tripartite model: II. Exploring the symptom structures of anxiety and depression in student, adult, and patient samples. *Journal of Abnormal Psychology, 104,* 15-25.

In: Psychology of Self-Control
Editors: A. Durante, et. al.

ISBN: 978-1-61470-881-0
© 2012 Nova Science Publishers, Inc.

Chapter 8

GIVING CHILDREN A PREFRONTAL CORTEX? INCREASED MENTAL CONTROL THROUGH EXTERNAL CUES

*Jae H. Paik[1], Hoan N. Luong[1] and Ezequiel Morsella[1,2]**

[1] Department of Psychology
San Francisco State University (SFSU)
1600 Holloway Avenue, EP 301
San Francisco, California, U. S.
[2] Department of Neurology
University of California, San Francisco, U. S.

Abstract

A form of self-control, mental control is essential for children to maintain focus in the classroom and not be distracted by irrelevant stimuli or thoughts. In adults, mental control can backfire, as in the case of *ironic processing*, in which one is more likely to think about something (e. g. , white bears) when instructed to not think about that thing. An interesting finding is that, though children (ages 7-9) can be easily distracted and experience undesired thoughts, they are not susceptible to ironic processing, making them an excellent population in which to study the

* Email address: morsella@sfsu. edu

benefits of increased mental control through external cues. We replicated the finding that children are immune from ironic processing, and provide evidence that external cues can increase children's mental control and can diminish their undesired thoughts. This finding begins to illuminate the complex liaisons among attention, set, self-control, and the development of the kinds of executive processes associated with prefrontal cortex.

INTRODUCTION

It is a common observation that children often fail to maintain "focus" (i. e. , sustained attention) in a classroom setting (Ackerman, 1987; Brodeur, 2004). Such failure may arise from multiple factors, including the inability to maintain'set' and suppress attention to task-irrelevant stimuli (Gazzaley, Cooney, Rissman, & D'Esposito, 2005; Ridderinkhof, van der Molen, & Band, 1997), including internal stimuli such as distracting thoughts (Morsella, Ben-Zeev, Lanska, & Bargh, 2010), the topic of this research project on children (ages 7-9). To regulate the occurrence of distracting thoughts, it is essential for the child to exert'mental control' (Gaskell, Wells, & Calam, 2001; Wegner, 1994). It is well established that, in adults, mental control sometimes backfires, as in the case of *ironic processing*, in which one is more likely to think about something (e. g. , white bears) when instructed to not think about that thing (Wegner, Schneider, Carter, & White, 1987; see review in Smári, 2001). In adults, the set to *not think of X* seems to activate to some extent the undesired content X (Wegner, 1994), leading to increased occurrences of the undesired thought. That one is more likely to think of a thought when attempting to suppress it has been referred to as the *immediate enhancement effect* (Gaskell et al. , 2001). This finding has important implications for the understanding of the liaisons among thought, obsessions (Wegner, 1994), and rumination (Nolen-Hoeksema, 1996).

Interestingly, previous research reveals that, though elementary school children (e. g. , of ages 7-9) do show difficulty in suppressing distraction and do experience undesired thoughts (Ackerman, 1987; Brodeur, 2004; Gaskell et al. , 2001), for some reason they are not susceptible to the immediate enhancement effect (Gaskell et al. , 2001). In fact, children show the opposite effect of what is found with adults: Children are better at suppressing an undesired thought when instructed to suppress it than when instructed to freely think about anything, including the undesired thought (Gaskell et al. , 2001). Thus, it could be said that, in this particular instance, children are more successful at cognitive control than adults. This intriguing finding may reflect that children lack the high-level set representations (or'metathoughts'; Wegner, 1994, p. 54) that, though beneficial in most forms of mental control, render adults susceptible to ironic processing. These representations are believed to be stored in frontal cortex (Grafman & Krueger, 2009), a brain structure that is known to not be fully developed in children. Because of their immunity from set-related effects in which mental control strategies backfire, children are an informative population in which to examine how the strengthening of set-related representations can influence mental control.

Recent research suggests that mental control can be influenced by the external stimuli composing one's current environment (Levine, Morsella, & Bargh, 2007). In such a situation, external stimuli can activate action-related sets (Levine et al. , 2007; Morsella, Larson, Zarolia, & Bargh, 2011) and can help hold information in mind, making the world a kind of'external memory' (O'Regan, 1992), in which some of the burden of mental control can be relegated (Brooks, 1991; Clark & Chalmers, 1998; Hoover & Richardson, 2008). Thus, perceptual stimuli arising from the external world (or even from one's own body) can be used as cues that facilitate mental control and cognitive processing more generally (Ballard, Hayhoe, Pook, & Rao, 1997; Goldin-Meadow, Nusbaum, Kelly, & Wagner, 2001; Morsella & Krauss, 2004).

In light of children's immunity toward ironic processing (Gaskell et al. , 2001), an important observation demanding additional empirical evidence, and in light of the power of external stimuli to influence mental control through set, we sought to evaluate the influence of external, set-related stimuli on children's mental control. In our study, school-age children participated in a variant (based on Gaskell et al. , 2001) of the classic thought-suppression experiment (Wegner et al. , 1987). As in the classic paradigm, in the suppression condition, participants were instructed to not think of something (a green rabbit; Gaskell et al. , 2001); in the control condition, they were instructed to think about anything including the target object (the green rabbit). Children then reported the occurrence of green rabbits through self-report (tapping on the table as each thought occurred). Because there is little research on ironic processing in children, we concluded that replicating Gaskell et al.'s (2001) finding would be an important contribution in its own right. If, as previous data suggest, children can successfully suppress more undesired thoughts when instructed to suppress thoughts than when instructed to freely think about anything (including the undesired content), then what else can improve their cognitive control during thought suppression?

With this in mind, to examine the influence of external stimuli on set and mental control, we included a new condition in our thought-suppression paradigm. In this "External Cue" condition, children sat in view of an external object that served to remind them of the instructions of the task. Children were simply told, "This object is to remind you to follow instructions. " Hypothesis 1 was that such a cue would actually increase mental control and decrease the occurrence of undesired thoughts, something that has never been demonstrated experimentally in children participating in a thought-suppression experiment. Hypothesis 2 was that such a cue would increase the activation of high-level set representations (or metathoughts; Wegner, 1994) and make children perform as adults do. This would be the first demonstration that increasing the activation of set renders children susceptible to the immediate enhancement effect. Either pattern of results would have implications for our understanding of the complex liaisons among set strength, attention, self-control in children (Mischel, Shoda, & Rodriguez, 1989), and the changes across the lifespan of the kinds of executive processes associated with prefrontal cortex. In addition, results from the external cue condition would illuminate the role of environmental cues in self-regulation (cf. , Wood, Quinn, & Kashy, 2002).

METHODS

Participants. A sample of 59 children ranging in age from 7 years 6 months to 9 years and 8 months (mean age = 8 years and 7. 8 months; SD = 9. 6 months) was recruited from elementary schools in the San Francisco Bay Area that served mid to upper middle-class population. An additional sample of 12 children were invited to participate but excluded from the study because they could not follow instructions.

Design, Setting, and Materials. Children were tested individually in a separate room at their participating school. Children sat opposite the experimenter at a table. We used a fully experimental, 2x2 within-subjects design, with the factor External Cue having two levels (Absent or Present) and Instruction having two levels (Suppress or Control). We adopted a pseudo-random design that met the following criteria. First, to avoid task-switching effects (Logan, 2009), participants should switch instructional set as few times as possible. Hence, the session consisted of two'mega-blocks,' one representing each level of the factor Instruction. The ordering of the Instruction levels was counterbalanced between participants. Two other rules pertained to the presentation of the levels of the factor External Cue. First, to simplify the experience of the subject, the first-half of the Suppress or Control conditions would be without the presence of the external cue, which could confuse the subjects after task switching. Second, each level of the factor External Cue should be presented for equal spans of time. For these two reasons, within each mega-block of the factor of Instruction, the External Cue Absent condition always preceded the External Cue Present condition. These were mini-blocks within the mega-blocks of the factor Instructions. Future studies may benefit from designs that are more fully-counterbalanced.

In the External Cue Present condition, children sat in view of a novel object (a thin 18 x 24 cm wooden screen atop a short stand; Figure 1), placed one-foot before them and occupying most of their visual field. Children were told, "This object is to remind you to follow instructions. " Care was taken to never mention anything associated with the undesired thought (the green rabbits).

Procedures. As in the Gaskell et al. (2001) study, children were first trained to tap the table upon experiencing a thought. To make sure that children knew how to perform this practice exercise, as in the Gaskell et al. (2001) study, children were asked to repeat back to the experimenter the instructions of the exercise. As in the Gaskell et al. (2001) study, children were able to perform this task.

For the experimental task, children first heard the story of a green rabbit (from Gaskell et al. , 2001) and then answered questions about the story. In the Suppress condition (lasting 2 minutes), children were then instructed to try not to think of green rabbits and to tap the table whenever they thought of a green rabbit. The Control condition was identical except that children were instructed to think of anything that they wanted to think about, including green rabbits. In the External Cue Absent condition, no object was placed before children; in the External Cue Present condition, the object was presented in front of participants. Our dependent measure was the number of taps as a function of condition.

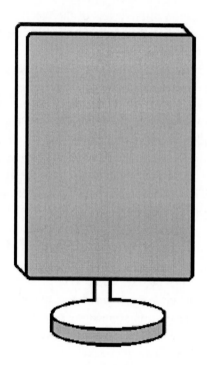

Figure 1. Schematic of the stimulus serving as the external cue. Not drawn to scale.

RESULTS

As illustrated in Figure 2 and consistent with Hypothesis 1, there was a main effect of External Cue in which there were fewer thoughts about green rabbits in the Present than Absent conditions, $F(1, 58) = 4.627, p < .05$ ($\eta_p^2 = .07$). Replicating the findings of Gaskell et al. (2001), there was also a main effect of Instruction, in which there were fewer thoughts about green rabbits in the Suppress than Control conditions, $F(1, 58) = 16.963, p < .001$ ($\eta_p^2 = .23$). There was no interaction between the factors External Cue and Instruction, $F(1, 58) = .638, p > .42$ ($\eta_p^2 = .01$).

Based Gaskell et al. (2001) study, we conducted a manipulation check in which, after each trial, children rated how often they thought of the green rabbit on a 1-to-5 Likert scale, ranging from 0 ("Not at all") to 5 ("Lots and lots"). The pattern of mean estimates reflected the general pattern displayed in

Figure 2, with a main effect of Instruction, $F(1, 58) = 23.723, p < .0001$, and External Cue, $F(1, 58) = 30.376, p < .0001$, and no interaction between the two factors, $F(1, 58) = 1.514, p = .22$.

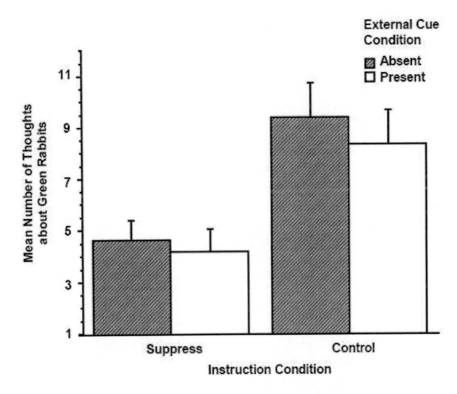

Figure 2. Mean number of thoughts about green rabbits as a function of instruction and external cue conditions.

This pattern of results corroborates that children were following instructions. One could argue that, because the order of presentation of the conditions was not fully randomized, the effect of External Cue could just be an artifact of a practice effect, in which subjects perform better as the session unfolds. To evaluate this possibility, we conducted an additional analysis of variance (ANOVA) in which we assessed whether there was an effect of the factor External Cue even when the factor mega-block order was taken into account. In this ANOVA 2 (Suppress or Control) x 2 (Present or Absent) x 2 (Suppress first or Control first) analysis, we replicated the aforementioned pattern of results, including the main effects of Instruction, $F(1, 57) = 29.018, p < .$

0001, and, importantly, External Cue, F (1, 57) = 4. 555, p < . 05. Although there was the expected main effect of the factor Block Order, F (1, 57) = 7. 294, p < . 01, the effect of External Cue was still statistically significant when taking this factor into account. This additional analysis suggests that time-at-task could not alone explain the effects of External Cue.

CONCLUSION

Consistent with Hypothesis 1 and with approaches (Ballard et al. , 1997; Brooks, 1991; Clark & Chalmers, 1998; Goldin-Meadow et al. , 2001; Levine et al. , 2007; Morsella et al. , 2011; Morsella & Krauss, 2004; O'Regan, 1992) proposing that external stimuli can play an important role in mental control, school-age children were best at suppressing undesired thoughts when they were instructed to suppress the thoughts and when an external cue reminded them to'follow instructions.' Hypothesis 2 was falsified: Any increased activation of set from the external cue did not appear to make children perform as adults do, with adults being more susceptible to the immediate enhancement effect. In contrast, the external object improved thought suppression. This provides an important replication of Gaskell et al. (2001) regarding the difference between ironic processing in children and adults.

Future investigations may benefit from designs that are more fully-counterbalanced and by focusing on the mechanisms by which the external cue improved performance in the Suppress condition. It may be that the effect resulted from children increasing their task-related concentration (cf. Lin & Wicker, 2007) or from children being distracted by the presence of the external object (cf. , Lin & Wicker, 2007; Wegner et al. , 1987; Experiment 2). The latter possibility is supported by the observation that the presence of the cue decreased thoughts in both the Suppress and Control conditions.

Regardless of the mechanism involved, this study is important because it replicates the important finding that children are more successful at decreasing an undesired mental content when instructed to do so than when instructed to think freely about anything, including the undesired content. It is well established that adults show the opposite effect, in which effortful suppression of a thought increases the occurrence of that thought (see review in Smári, 2001). In addition, the study demonstrates for the first time that external stimuli can be used innocuously to increase the mental control abilities of children in a circumstance as challenging as that of the Suppress condition.

Building on classic research showing that self-control at a young age predicts improved adaptive behavior during adolescence (e. g. , Mischel et al. , 1989), this initial finding of the effects of external stimuli on the mental control of children begins to illuminate the complex liaisons among set strength, attention, self-control in children, and the development of the kinds of executive processes associated with prefrontal cortex (Grafman & Kreuger, 2009). The basic finding has implications for our understanding of the complex liaisons among set strength, attention, self-control in children (Mischel, Shoda, & Rodriguez, 1989), and the changes across the lifespan of the kinds of executive processes associated with prefrontal cortex. At a minimum, we replicated the important finding by Gaskell et al. (2001) that, for some reason, children are not susceptible to the immediate enhancement effect experienced by adult participants (see review in Smári, 2001). Replicating this intriguing finding is an important contribution in its own right.

REFERENCES

Ackerman, B. P. (1987). Selective attention and distraction in context-interactive situations in children and adults. *Journal of Experimental Child Psychology, 44,* 126-146.

Ballard, D. H. , Hayhoe, M. M. , Pook, P. K. , & Rao, R. P. (1997). Deictic codes for the embodiment of cognition. *Behavioral and Brain Sciences, 20,* 723-767.

Brodeur, D. A. (2004). Age changes in attention control: Assessing the role of stimulus contingencies. *Cognitive Development, 19,* 241-252.

Brooks, R. A. (1991). Intelligence without representation. *Artificial Intelligence, 47,* 139-159.

Clark, A. , & Chalmers, D. J. (1998). The extended mind. *Analysis, 58,* 7-19.

Gaskell, S. L. , Wells, A. , & Calam, R. (2001). An experimental investigation of thought suppression and anxiety in children. *British Journal of Clinical Psychology, 40,* 45-56.

Gazzaley, A. , Cooney, J. W. , Rissman, J. , & D'Esposito, M. (2005). Top-down suppression deficit underlies working memory impairment in normal aging. *Nature Neuroscience, 8,* 1298-1300.

Goldin-Meadow, S. , Nusbaum, H. , Kelly, S. , & Wagner, S. (2001). Explaining math: Gesturing lightens the load. *Psychological Science, 12*(6), 516-522.

Grafman, J. , & Kreuger, F. (2009). The prefrontal cortex stores structured event complexes that are the representational basis for intentional actions. In E. Morsella, J. A. Bargh, & P. Gollwitzer (Eds.), *Oxford handbook of human action* (pp. 119-213). New York: Oxford University Press.

Hoover, M. A. , & Richardson, D. C. (2008). When facts go down the rabbit hole: Contrasting features and objecthood as indexes to memory. *Cognition, 108,* 533-542.

Levine, L. R. , Morsella, E. , & Bargh, J. A. (2007). The perversity of inanimate objects: Stimulus control by incidental musical notation. *Social Cognition, 25,* 265-280.

Lin, Y-J. , & Wicker, F. (2007). A comparison of the effects of thought suppression, distraction and concentration. *Behavior Research and Therapy, 45,* 2924-2937.

Logan, G. D. (2008). The role of memory in the control of action. In E. Morsella, J. A. Bargh, & P. M. Gollwitzer (Eds.), *Oxford handbook of human action* (pp. 427-441). New York: Oxford University Press.

Mischel, W. , Shoda, Y. , & Rodriguez. (1989). Delay of gratification in children. *Science, 244,* 933-938.

Morsella, E. , Ben-Zeev, A. , Lanska, M. , & Bargh, J. A. (2010). The spontaneous thoughts of the night: How future tasks breed intrusive cognitions. *Social Cognition, 28,* 640-649.

Morsella, E. , & Krauss, R. M. (2004). The role of gestures in spatial working memory and speech. *American Journal of Psychology, 117,* 411-424.

Morsella, E. , Larson, L. R. L. , Zarolia, P. , & Bargh, J. A. (2011). Stimulus control: The sought or unsought influence of the objects we tend to. *Psicólogica: International Journal of Methodology and Experimental Psychology, 32,* 145-170.

Nolen-Hoeksema, S. (1996). Chewing the cud and other ruminations. The automaticity of everyday life. In R. S. Wyer (Ed.), *Advances in social cognition* (Vol. 9, pp. 226-244). Mahwah, NJ: Erlbaum.

O'Regan, J. K. (1992). Solving the'real' mysteries of visual perception: The world as an outside memory. *Canadian Journal of Psychology, 46,* 461-488.

Ridderinkhof, K. R. , van der Molen, M. W. , Band, G. P. H. , & Bashore, T. R. (1997). Sources of interference from irrelevant information: A developmental study. *Journal of Experimental Child Psychology, 65,* 315-341.

Smári, J. (2001). Fifteen years of suppression of white bears and other thoughts: What are the lessons for obsessive-compulsive disorder research and treatment? *Scandinavian Journal of Behavior Therapy, 30,* 147-160.

Wegner, D. M. (1994). *White bears and other unwanted thoughts: Suppression, obsession, and the psychology of mental control.* New York: Guilford.

Wegner, D. M. , Schneider, D. J. , Carter, S. R. , & White, T. L. (1987). Paradoxical effects of thought suppression. *Journal of Personality and Social Psychology, 53,* 5-13.

Wood, W. , Quinn, J. , & Kashy, D. (2002). Habits in everyday life: Thought, emotion, and action. *Journal of Personality and Social Psychology, 83,* 1281-1297.

INDEX